Rapid Probler

RPR®: A Problem Diagnosis Method
for IT Professionals

Paul Offord

Advance Seven Limited, Essex, England

Customer Services
Advance Seven Limited
Melville House
High Street
Great Dunmow
Essex CM6 1AF
United Kingdom

Phone: +44 1371 876805
Email: info@advance7.com

Published by Advance Seven Limited

ISBN: 978-1-4478-4443-3

First printing September 2011

Second impression

Preface

Target Audience

The principles of RPR can be used to solve any IT problem and so the method has wide appeal, particularly to 3rd Line Support, 4th Line Support and Supplier Support people. Those businesses that have adopted ITIL as the framework for delivering IT Services will find RPR to be a natural fit within Service Operations.

Conventions

Throughout this manual you'll see:

	Cool tip
	Ideas to save time or improve effectiveness.

	Anecdote
	Real life experiences that reinforce the point being made.

	Key point
	Statements that relate to fundamental principles of the RPR method.

Language

Use of ITIL Terminology

This manual uses ITIL terminology wherever possible, although you'll spot exceptions to this rule throughout. A term of particular note is 'problem'. References are often made to problem (with a lower case 'p') whereas strict ITIL terminology may be Event or Incident. Sticking strictly to these latter phrases seems unnatural. For example, a user rarely calls the Service Desk and says "I've had an Event", or "I've just had an Incident on my PC", and so the word 'problem' is used liberally.

Tools and Technologies

This manual occasionally refers to certain tools and technologies. RPR is not proscriptive and so the use of other tools or the application to other technologies makes no difference to the RPR process or success rate. The reason for referring to specific tools and technologies is that it's preferable to explain the method through specific examples which can then be easily adapted to other situations than to write something vague in an attempt to cover all possibilities.

Manual Structure

This manual is divided into *parts* which contain *sections* which in turn contain *subsections*.

Gender

Throughout this manual, for easy reading, the words 'he' or 'she' have been used when referring to a person. This doesn't assume a specific gender for a specific role.

Trademarks

All terms used in this book that are known to be trade or service marks have been capitalised, although Advance Seven Limited cannot guarantee the accuracy of such references. Any reference to a trade or service mark does not affect its validity.

RPR® is a registered trademark of Advance Seven Limited.

Table of Contents

Table of Figures

Introduction

Background

The need for a structured approach to problem investigation and diagnosis is being driven by four factors:

- A relentless pressure to reduce IT operational spend

- Increasingly sophisticated needs, increased system interconnection and integrated business applications have made computer systems more complex and subject to very complicated problems

- The drive for increased business efficiency increasing the demand for consistent application performance and stability

- The increased complexity of technical support that may include enterprise, Internet, outsourced and cloud elements

Whilst traditional problem diagnosis techniques have served us well up till now, IT support people are struggling with an increasing volume of difficult problems.

Rapid Problem Resolution (RPR$^{®}$) is a method that has much to offer in this area. The method isn't new, in fact it has been practised continuously and successfully since 1990. What is relatively new is its wide public availability.

The Core Process has been revised eleven times since it was first documented, and the Supporting Techniques are being continuously updated to keep pace with information and communication technologies. The principle difference between RPR and other methods is that RPR is an IT-based method specifically designed for IT people. As opposed to a generic and purely theoretical method, the Supporting Techniques of RPR make it very practical and relate directly to the IT components that are found in every business.

RPR produces impressive results. It cuts the IT workload associated with complex problems by 47% and corresponding downtime by 64%[1].

New in v2.xx

If you've attended RPR training based on a release earlier than version 2, or even the Advance Network Troubleshooting courses that were run by Advance7 in the mid-90s, you'll notice a significant change to the method.

The five-step procedure present in earlier versions has been totally replaced with a nineteen-step process. Each process step has a checklist to validate the quality of its execution.

The introduction of the RPR Core Process has enabled us to separate the sequence of activities from the techniques used in the practice of RPR, which is an important step for future development as we will see below.

Despite all the changes, you'll recognise the principles underpinning the method and many of the Supporting Techniques.

New in v2.03

The major change in v2.03 is the complete separation of the Supporting Techniques. The RPR Core Process has been refined with each release, but the changes are not fundamental and the process rarely needs to be changed.

Of course, technology is moving very quickly and new Supporting Techniques are being continuously developed to meet the new challenges. For this reason the principle source for the Supporting Techniques will be the RPRsupport.com website (under development at the time of writing). However, some key generic Supporting Techniques are included here to enable the reader to gain immediate benefit from RPR.

---

[1] Based on the analysis of 100 problems investigated using RPR – see http://www.advance7.com/info/factsheets/RprStatistics.pdf

The Supporting Techniques section is organised so that the reader can reference each technique without having to flip back and forth through the book. This has led to some duplication of information between sections.

Organisation of This Manual

Part 1 provides an introduction to the method and some of its fundamental principles. Specifically we look at:

- RPR Scope – describing the types of problems that RPR addresses

- Grey Problems – describing a particular type of problem and the challenges it poses

- State of the Art – describing the informal and formal methods that are currently in use

- Problem Investigation in Practice – outlining current thinking and common practice

- RPR Overview – outlining the RPR Approach

- RPR in Practice – describing how RPR can be integrated into IT operations and the skills it needs

- Coexistence with Other Methods – describing how RPR complements and supplements other popular methods

- RPR Concepts – both industry and RPR concepts that form the foundation of RPR

Part 2 defines each step of the method, with a common set of subsections of:

- Objectives
- Activities
- Supporting Techniques
- Checklist
- Next Process Step

Part 3 describes a number of key Supporting Techniques that help technical staff achieve the objectives of each step of the process.

Part 4 presents some essential Soft Skills to help managers, team leaders and others deal with the people aspects of using a problem diagnosis method.

Essential Reading

Much of the text in the first part of this manual can be skim-read or skipped, although there are some sections and subsections that you should consider as essential reading. These introduce terminology and concepts that are used in the definition of the Core Process and the Supporting Techniques.

The essential sections are:

Section	Page
Grey Problems	
All sections	10
RPR Overview	
Principles	28
Process	30
Limitations and Demands	33
RPR Concepts	
Root Cause	43
Definitive Diagnostic Data	54
Functional Units and Protocols	57
Fault Domain	59
Typical Diagnostic Capture and RCI Scenario	63

RPR Practitioners Forum

Although this book includes details of the essential RPR Supporting Techniques, there are more, and the list is growing. Prior to the availability of the RPRsupport.com website, you can receive details of these additional techniques by joining the RPR Practitioners forum on LinkedIn (www.linkedin.com). At the time of printing, there is no charge for this forum.

RPR Scope

To assess the scope of RPR, in this section we characterise a problem in two different ways:

- Problem Symptom Category – the user's perception of the problem

- Problem Complexity – related to frequency and knowledge of the causing technology

Problem Symptom Category

The symptoms of a problem fall into one of four groups:

- Design – the system doesn't work the way the user wants it to

- Functionality – the system should work but it doesn't and produces either:

  - an error message, OR

  - incorrect output

- Stability – the system works most of the time but sometimes fails and produces either:

  - an error message, OR

  - incorrect output

- Performance – the system works OK but is sometimes or always slow

The problem may not be an end-user issue, it could be purely operational. For example, an error message may repeatedly appear in a system log even though there have been no related complaints from users.

RPR is intended to deal with functionality, stability and performance issues, although it is mostly used for the last two.

Problem Frequency

Problem managers will aim to identify the root cause of:

- One-off Problems – typically identified as the result of a Major Incident

- Ongoing Problems – that the users are experiencing right now

- Recurring Problems – that cause repeated incidents with similar symptoms

RPR provides a way to identify the root cause of Ongoing or Recurring Problems. ITIL refers to these as "ongoing recurring problems". Here we refer to the two categories separately to indicate that an Ongoing Problem is continuous whereas a Recurring Problem is intermittent i.e. there are periods of correct operation mixed with problem periods.

Combining the frequency with causing technology information, we can gain a view of the complexity of the problem and hence determine the difficulty of investigating it.

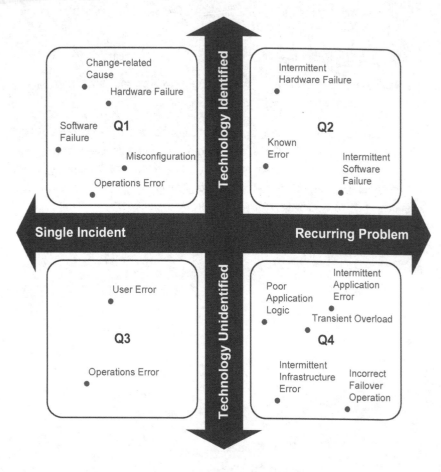

Figure 1 Problem complexity

Q1 – In a typical IT department 80 to 90% of problems are solid faults that are easily tracked down to a causing technology. The appropriate technical or platform support team efficiently deals with these problems every day.

Q2 – Some recurring problems are due to a Known Error, or are obviously being caused by a particular hardware or software component. These problems are typically handled by technical support people working with suppliers.

Q3 – Every so often a one-off problem occurs, and the cauoo of these may never be found.

Q4 – Problems in this quadrant cause a disproportionately high adverse impact on business efficiency, IT service levels, staff morale, IT workload and personal KPIs. The technical ownership for these issues is unclear and so we refer to them as 'grey problems' i.e. not black or white.

RPR deals with ongoing and recurring problems (those problems in Q2 and Q4), and is ideal for finding the root cause of grey problems (Q4).

Grey Problems

Dangers

Grey problems are typically assessed as mid to low priority and if not resolved quickly are put on the 'too difficult to deal with' stack. This can be dangerous as low-level, ongoing and recurring problems can be an early warning of bigger problems to come. Not dealing with them is likely to result in one or more of the following:

- The problem grows with business load until a tipping point is reached when it causes a Major Incident

- Ongoing and recurring problems create a fog that makes it more difficult to solve all other problems

- The existence of ongoing recurring low-priority problems closes out IT options – "I'd rather we didn't expand use of the XYZ system because it's already creaking", etc.

- Users are ground down by the constant low-level problems and this causes dissatisfaction with the IT service

A business will accept the big one-off incidents – they know that occasional failures are inevitable – but constant low-level problems frustrate users and introduce business inefficiencies as work practices are adjusted to cope.

Because the causing component and even the technology are unknown, the problem bounces between technical support teams.

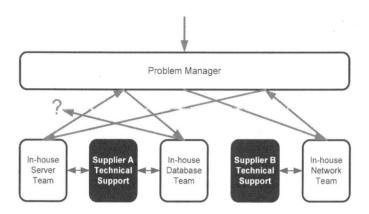

Figure 2   Grey problems

Without a problem diagnosis method, progress towards resolution is very haphazard, and no one is ever quite sure how close the team is to finding the solution. The team may get lucky and find the problem tomorrow or it may drag on for another month.

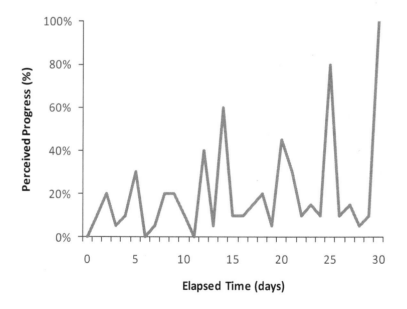

Figure 3   Perceived progress

This causes frustration for the users as they watch IT support teams pursue a seemingly endless stream of theories with no end in sight. IT support people and managers also become frustrated as the associated workload increases. A grey problem may take weeks, months or even years to fix – in fact it may never be fixed.

Where the business case for resolution cannot be justified, the problem may simply be recorded as a 'known error'. This may be reasonable if the business impact is low, although it is still preferable to understand the root cause to avoid confusion with other problems and assess how the impact may grow.

Problem Priorities

There are links between ongoing and recurring problems, grey problems and non-urgent problems in that:

- Many ongoing and recurring problems are grey
- Many ongoing and recurring problems are at the priority 3 and 4 end of the list
- Few support teams find the time to tackle the 3s and 4s

Characteristics

The typical characteristics of a grey problem situation are:

- The frequency of Service Desk calls about the problem steadily reduces
- Business adjusts its work processes to accommodate the problem
- Troubleshooting activity is unstructured and tends to be driven by 'gut-feel', anecdote or theory
- There is no sense of direction in the problem resolution effort
- An ever-growing group of people get involved

- Suppliers may:
  - wait for proof that it's their problem
  - resort to swap-out
  - blamo someone else, OR
  - suggest an upgrade
- Repeated statements that, "We want to try one more thing" are heard
- Time and money is wasted on upgrades or a Service Improvement Programme with no clear understanding of how or why it will resolve the problem
- Health checks are proposed
- Progress towards a resolution is slow and unpredictable

 What next?

A financial services company had suffered a problem for eight months where users intermittently lost access to networked applications. IT support was outsourced to a company with well-defined procedures for handling problems but the situation had become serious. The IT Director called the outsource company's Service Manager in for a crisis meeting:-

ITD: 'What do you plan to do next?'
SM: 'We've invoked the Red Team.'
ITD: 'OK, what will they do?'
SM: 'They are experts in this area.'
ITD: 'Yes, but what will they actually do?'
SM: 'Well they have access to specialist equipment.'
ITD: 'But you're not telling me what they plan to do.'

Silence.

Intermittent Problems and Transient Events

It's worth noting the connection between an intermittent problem and a transient event. An intermittent problem is one that cannot be easily reproduced and is therefore unpredictable. Many performance problems are intermittent and may be caused by a transient event – something that is there one minute and gone the next.

For example, an intermittent response time problem could be caused by a transient database overload. Transient overloads are often not detected by monitoring systems and so the causing technology is not easily identified.

State of the Art

Popular Informal Methods

In this subsection we look at some of the popular methods that are used, often successfully for the early phases of a problem, and their shortcomings.

Test Procedures and Checklists

This approach forms the backbone of the diagnostic work carried out by Service Desk and First-Line Support staff, and realistically it's the only process based method that makes sense at the early stages of the problem. Success relies on the problem being known or at least predictable under certain circumstances or configurations. The majority of incidents dealt with by the IT Operations Support staff are handled in this way.

Review Recent Changes

It is estimated that 85% of all problems arise from change. Therefore it makes good sense to determine when the problem started and review the changes that took place just before the first incidents were reported.

Even this logical approach may not determine the cause of a problem. There may be a time lag between the change causing incidents, or the incidents being reported by users, and the effect of a change is not always fully understood. The information recorded in an Incident Record may also be less than perfect.

Simple Trial and Error

This is an approach that is often presented as 'past experience' or as 'based on knowledge of the product'. Furthermore, the arguments supporting a recommended change or upgrade can seem very persuasive, but are often not based upon known root cause. In reality this approach is no more than trial and error.

Despite its shortcomings, trial and error has its place. It may not be ideal but it is a pragmatic approach to 2nd and 3rd Line Support investigation and is a practical way to test a theory, provided that any change can be limited to a test environment, a test user or, at most, a small control group.

Process of Elimination

A process of elimination is often used by 2nd Line Support, 3rd Line Support and Supplier Support teams, and is based on the assumption that an unknown piece of equipment (or perhaps software) is faulty. Equipment or software is swapped out in a controlled manner to identify the offending component. The disadvantages of this method are:

- It doesn't establish the root cause and so the change may just mask the problem, which often returns later as the pattern of usage changes

- The swapping of equipment or software often creates new problems

- You can never be sure if the appearance of a new, but similar symptom is due to the original cause, or related to a new issue caused by the swap out

- This approach does not identify or deal with a misconfiguration problem

- It cannot be used effectively to identify a problem with a service such as a managed network

- The method is slow

- The method can be expensive if new equipment has to be purchased

Pattern Method

Pattern methods rely on gathering large amounts of information about the users affected and equipment in use (job function, location, PC spec, OS, time of day, whether problem occurred after a change, pattern of work, etc.) and trying to establish a pattern.

This is a widely-used approach and can be successful. However, pattern methods require a detailed and accurate record of the problem, and in a busy IT department this is often not available. IT staff may use very sophisticated pattern method spreadsheets to analyse a difficult problem but this method still remains unreliable.

The success and weaknesses of this method are much the same as those of a straightforward trial and error approach. The disadvantages are:

- It doesn't directly identify the root cause and any resulting change may just mask the problem, which often returns later

- Because the root cause is not explicitly identified, any change may cause a new problem

- You can never be sure if the appearance of a new, but similar symptom is due to the original cause or related to a new cause due to the change

- The method fails if a problem has multiple causes

- The method fails if the input information is imperfect, and it very often is

- The method is slow

A key advantage of pattern-based methods is that they can be used to help determine the cause of problems that do not recur, something for which RPR is not best suited.

Statistical Method

The Statistical Method is typically based on the study of large amounts of data and looks at the system 'as a whole'. Statistical data for resource utilisation and error rates is gathered, often over prolonged periods such as a week or month. The data is then analysed and inferences are drawn. Whilst this method works reasonably well when there is a very obvious overload or excessive error condition (which is usually spotted at an early stage), it almost always fails in all other cases because you can't state categorically that at the time user X had the problem 'this' is what went wrong. For this reason, a statistical approach more often than not leads to a totally wrong conclusion.

Despite this weakness this method is very widely used, and much favoured by suppliers and consultants.

However, this method has so many disadvantages that it should be used sparingly. Use it to check for an obvious cause, but turn to other methods if it doesn't produce results quickly.

Health Check

The IT department may choose to perform a health check or audit of the IT infrastructure supporting an application in the belief that they will discover the cause of a problem. The statistical techniques outlined above often form part of the work and so the approach suffers from the same weaknesses. These projects are often large, complex, last a long time and will always identify issues. Unfortunately, it's common for the issues found to have nothing to do with the problem being investigated. Much time and money is spent addressing the issues that are identified, only to find that the problem persists.

Whilst a health check is useful to measure capacity headroom and the rate of underlying errors that are not service impacting, it's rarely effective as a problem diagnosis method.

Lies, damn lies and statistics

An investment bank launched a service to deliver research data to customers via the Internet but ever since going live, customers had reported intermittent performance problems. A management consultancy had spent three months analysing the problem and produced a 250-page PowerPoint presentation.

The presentation had a myriad of facts and figures, with fascinating graphs and diagrams. In summary, the conclusions and recommendations said:

- SSL acceleration might cut response times by 5s

- Faster processors in the web servers might reduce response times by 1s

- More data is needed to determine further recommendations

They certainly didn't need more data, they were awash with it. By restructuring the investigation using RPR the two causes were found within 3 days:

- A bug in the software of a load balancer was causing slow performance

- Users were sometimes connected to a mirror site in New York which was backed up during the UK morning

It was also possible to prove categorically that SSL acceleration would only cut response times by 150 ms and that there was no problem with web server capacity.

Other Formal Method

There are many formal methods available:- ITIL cites several. Although some have sprung from the IT industry, many of the front-runners are actually adaptations of business problem-resolution methods. Typical shortcomings are:

- Due to the 'soft' nature of many business problems, methods with this lineage are not designed to take advantage of the logic and tools available to us in the IT industry

- Many of the 'methods' are in fact just processes with no supporting IT techniques making it difficult for IT people to run the process

- Many methods require that you already know the root cause as one of a list of possible causes that are then tested

- To avoid disruption, some methods force the IT team to try to recreate the problem in a lab environment, which is time consuming, expensive, and in the case of grey problems, rarely works

- Many methods are based on the identification of a pattern of occurrences of symptoms, and whilst this approach has its uses, pattern-based methods are quite unreliable

- Many methods rely on statistical analysis which often fails with grey problems due to their intermittent nature and transient causes

- Some methods rely on trial and error or at least a process of elimination

As with pattern-based methods in general, many of these methods can be useful in trying to determine the root cause of a problem that is neither ongoing nor recurring. The complementary nature of RPR and other methods is covered in greater detail in *Coexistence with Other Methods* on page 37.

Problem Investigation in Practice

Typical Scenario

The technical support function of an IT department is traditionally organised into specialist Technical Support Teams (Platform and Application Support). In large organisations these teams may have considerable knowledge of a technology, sometimes on a par with those of their suppliers, although this level of specialism may come at a price:

- Silos of specialisation often struggle to communicate with one another

- KPIs for the team are centred on the performance of their own technologies

- The silo philosophy may also be reinforced by the outsourcing of certain functions

On balance, the specialised technical support team is probably still the best model for medium to large organisations as it enables IT Operations to complete regular tasks quickly and solve non-grey problems. However, it works less well when handling a grey problem, which will often be thrown between the silos like the proverbial hot potato.

The ITIL Model

ITIL tries to help here by defining the role of the Problem Manager who has an end-to-end responsibility and access that spans the specialist teams. ITIL suggests that where necessary, members of the various Technical Support Teams are seconded to a Problem Solving Group.

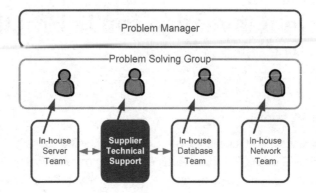

Figure 4   ITIL problem solving group

Unfortunately, although the Problem Manager may pull together a Problem Solving Group from the Technical Support Teams, coordinate resources and provide necessary reports, he or she rarely directs problem diagnosis activity. Very few problem management functions have matured to the point where problem managers take an active role in problem diagnosis.

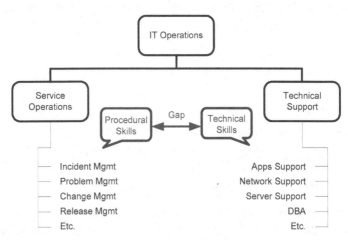

Figure 5   Effectiveness gap

This results in a gap between the Problem Manager and each member of the PSG causing the team to fail to gel and eventually everyone reverts to focusing on attempting to prove that their particular technology is not to blame.

Predictably, each team produces convincing evidence that their technology is not the cause of the problem. Such proof needs to be treated with some scepticism since it is not possible to prove conclusively that something is not the cause of a problem if you haven't determined the actual cause.

ITIL documentation is weak in the area of Problem Investigations and Diagnosis; the subject is covered in little more than two pages.

RPR Overview

Benefits

RPR is an effective way to find the root cause of any ongoing recurring problem, including grey problems where the component or causing technology is unknown. Advance7 used RPR for the first time in August 1990 to resolve a remote connectivity problem. The power of the method was obvious from the outset when a problem that had afflicted the business for 17 weeks was solved in one day. Over the intervening years RPR has been practiced, developed and refined through resolving problems in a wide range of business and public sector environments.

RPR was designed from the outset to solve IT problems and is heavily influenced by software engineering techniques. Given this starting point, RPR avoids the shortcomings suffered by other methods. Its strengths come from several key features:

- RPR is an evidence-based process in that it identifies a problem's root cause, measures it and provides absolute proof that it has been addressed by any fix applied, which makes the method completely reliable

- It makes full use of the IT tools that are available in every business which makes it a faster method than those that do not use this advantage

- It's a fully mature method with a clear process and supporting techniques making it easier for support staff to use

- RPR requires no pre-conceived idea of the cause of the problem, in fact such thoughts are positively discouraged, and this avoids time wasted in pursuing misguided theories

- The method generally uses non-disruptive techniques, so there is minimal business impact

- RPR doesn't require recreation in a lab environment, nor even testing outside of normal working hours, both of which are time consuming, can be expensive and often fail

- The method is based around the collection of Definitive Diagnostic Data[2] at the exact point of a problem and so identifies the cause precisely; transient or not

- Due to the creation and use of definitive diagnostics, RPR identifies inaccurate input information and so is immune to such inaccuracies

- RPR is a collaborative method that enhances the skills of the IT Support Team and support companies, making it politically acceptable, job enhancing and again cutting the fix time

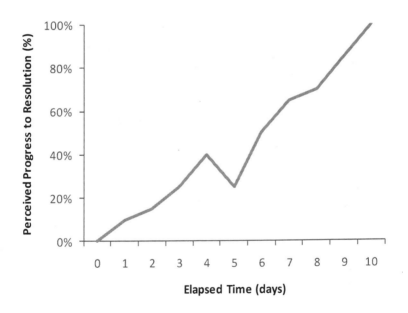

Figure 6 Progress with RPR

---

[2] Definitive diagnostics play a major role in RPR. The meaning of definitive diagnostics and the actions required to generate them is covered at some length later in Definitive Diagnostic Data on page 44.

As the above chart shows, progress with RPR is more predictable. The RPR Core Process ensuroo that problem diagnosis is deterministic. There will be setbacks but actual progress is known and all involved know what is to happen next. Compare this with *Figure 3   Perceived progress* on page 11.

When to Use RPR

Functional Escalation

RPR is not intended for initial investigation of a problem but for use when traditional techniques have been exhausted.

Problem Manager, PSG & 4th Line Support	● Investigate with RPR
3rd Line	● Check for overload ● Investigate with diagnostic tools ● Liaise with supplier tech support ● Review design
2nd Line	● Check monitoring systems ● Review recent changes ● Check for misconfiguration ● Check supplier knowledgebase
1st Line	● Check for misuse ● Check for known error
Service Desk	● Check for user error ● Check for PC fault

Figure 7   Functional escalation

Functional Escalation is an ITIL term referring to the escalation of a problem through 1st, 2nd and 3rd Line support. Grey problems are typical of issues that move through the functional escalation phases but remain undiagnosed. There are also two tell-tale phrases that indicate that the IT team is struggling with a grey problem:

"We are just going to try one more thing"

"We made some changes and things have improved a bit
but we still have some work to do"

At this point a structured approach should be adopted. Whether RPR is chosen or another method, a method-based approach will be faster and more reliable.

Other triggers for RPR are:

- Support people shy away from the problem and find reasons to pursue other problems or tasks

- The problem bounces from one Technical Support Team to another, each having checked their technology and declaring it not to be the cause

- A proposal that the problem should be diagnosed by conducting a health check

- Supplier support people are unwilling to take ownership of the problem

- When planning the next set of actions there is a prolonged discussion about what might or might not be causing the problem

- Support people look for patterns between symptoms and incidents hoping to find a common denominator

In such circumstances it's prudent to switch to RPR for faster resolution.

	Change for the sake of change?
	Don't try simply to change your way out of a problem. When something doesn't work properly there is often a temptation to change release, change technology, change anything. This is very risky if you don't know the original cause of the problem. One danger is that you introduce new problems, and after resolving those you are still left with the original problem.

4th Line Support

Some IT departments have a 4th Line Support function, although it is not always clear how their activity differs from that of 3rd Line. Use of a structured problem diagnosis method is an ideal differentiator for 4th Line support people.

Principles

There are three cornerstones of RPR:

- Each run of the process focuses on one symptom

- Diagnostic data that can be directly correlated to the user's problem (called Definitive Diagnostic Data) is gathered for individual instances of the symptom

- Changes made are based on the findings of analysis of the Definitive Diagnostic Data

The most striking difference from other methods is the first principle; the focus on one symptom. This is completely opposite to the traditional approach of looking for commonality between multiple symptoms.

RPR includes the use of a number of innovative techniques and it is worth highlighting two that are key to success:

- Establishing an accurate timeline of events

- The generation and use of markers to enable correlation of diagnostic data and user events

Process

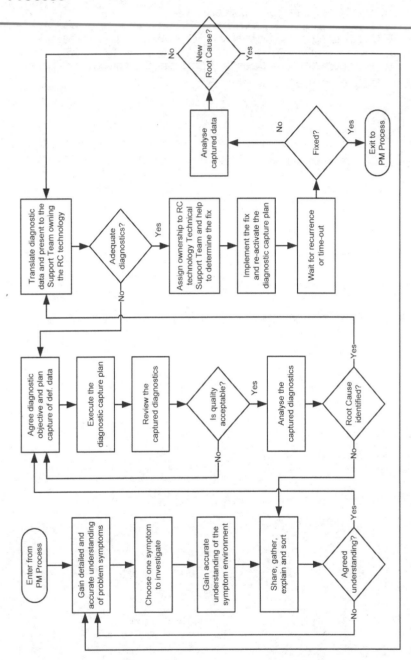

At a high level, the RPR Process has three phases:

- Discover

  - Gather and review existing information
  - Reach an agreed understanding of the problem

- Investigate

  - Create and execute a Diagnostic Capture Plan (DCP)
  - Analyse the results and iterate if necessary
  - Identify root cause

- Fix

  - Translate diagnostic data
  - Determine and implement a fix
  - Confirm root cause has been addressed

Process Step Structure

Each step of the Core Process is clearly defined by:

- Purpose
- Objectives
- Activities
- Supporting Techniques
- Checklist
- Next Process Step

This process makes RPR more controllable and more predictable than other approaches to problem diagnosis. All stakeholders know the current status of problem diagnosis and what needs to happen next.

The RPR Core Process describes what needs to be done and when. RPR Supporting Techniques describe how to achieve the objectives of each Core Process step, which means that technical support people quickly become effective RPR practitioners. The quality of execution of each step is monitored and controlled through a set of check points that form quality gates.

RPR is IT-specific, which means that the Supporting Techniques are based around the tools and techniques that already exist in every IT department. This makes for easy integration into IT operations.

RPR is a totally evidence-based method so there is no need for subjective judgements or speculation as to the possible causes. The result is faster Root Cause Identification and the elimination of risks associated with 'trying a fix'.

Integration into IT Operations

RPR is ITIL aligned. This means that it neatly dovetails into ITIL processes and provides the all important link between service-focused people (Service Delivery Managers, Recovery Managers, Incident Managers and Problem Managers) and technology-focused platform teams. RPR improves the communication between the groups, which leads to a more cohesive team.

RPR is primarily intended to deal with grey problems and so builds upon existing activities rather than replaces them. In ITIL terms, RPR is completely relevant to Problem Management, and slots into the *Problem Investigation and Diagnosis* section of ITIL v3.

	Non-ITIL
	Although RPR is ITIL-aligned it can just as easily be adopted in a non-ITIL environment. There are no organisational prerequisites to the adoption of RPR.

RPR deals very specifically with technical IT problems that are ongoing or recurring. Other methods are useful to investigate one-off Incidents and non-technical causes such as a procedure weakness, shortage of a specific skill and supplier contractual issues. RPR sits neatly alongside these and in some cases can fit as a sub-process within them if needed. See *Coexistence with Other Methods* on 39.

Limitations and Demands

It's worth noting the limitations and demands of RPR:

- Changes must not be made immediately prior to and/or whilst investigating the problem. Any change that affects the system being studied will invalidate the diagnostic data collection.

- RPR requires the users to suffer the problem at least one more time. The method is totally evidence-based and that means collecting the diagnostic data when the problem occurs.

- RPR can only deal with one symptom at a time. This is often controversial as there can be a belief that this is a slower method than taking an all-encompassing approach to determining a common cause.

- RPR is very difficult to use if you do not have an end-to-end view of a system e.g. if you are a network service provider with no ability to correlate the user's experience directly with your diagnostic data.

- IT Management must allow the problem solving group adequate dedicated time for problem analysis and during the data collection phase.

If not everyone involved understands or believes in the method, some of these issues can be difficult to overcome.

RPR in Practice

Enhancement of ITIL

Although ITIL provides a clear problem management process it provides little guidance regarding problem investigation and diagnosis. RPR deals with this ITIL shortcoming by:

- Providing the Problem Manager with a Core Process to drive the diagnosis effort

- Providing Supporting Techniques so that the Technical Support Teams can deliver the information needed

- Improving the speed and quality of technical communications between the teams

- Improving the speed and quality of communications to the business

RPR bridges the gap between the service- and technology-orientated teams by providing a problem investigation and diagnosis process and supporting techniques that can be understood by both sides.

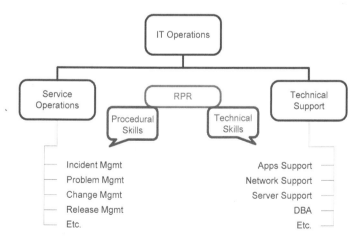

Figure 8 Bridging the gap

In practice, RPR will slot neatly into any IT organisation.

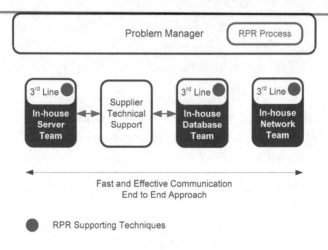

Figure 9   RPR in an IT Department

The figure above shows the Problem Manager as the person responsible for running the RPR Core Process but it could equally be a:

- Problem Manager

- Incident Manager

- Recovery Manager

- Service Delivery Manager

- Technical Team Leader

- 3rd Line Support Engineer

- Supplier Support Engineer

Ideally a Problem Manager should coordinate the activities of a Problem Solving Group. In practice a wide range of people take on this responsibility.

Ideal Skill Set

Whilst a Problem Manager is responsible for managing the process and activity, the technical leadership of diagnosis and resolution activity will probably be provided by a technical member of the Problem Solving Group. Ideal PSG members are senior people from the technical support teams with additional skills and experience including:

- A broad knowledge of IT and a good understanding of the fundamental technologies

- Confidence and ability to step outside the comfort zone of their own specialist area

- Strong analytical skills with a methodical approach to solving problems

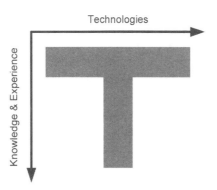

Figure 10   T-shaped people

Such people are often referred to as 'T-shaped' i.e. they have a strong broad IT knowledge but a deep understanding of one or more technologies.

Problem Analyst

Throughout this manual you'll find references to the role of Problem Analyst. This role is not defined in ITIL and individual organisations have their own definitions for this role. For the purposes of this manual, Problem Analyst refers to a member of the Problem Solving Group who has:

- RPR skills

- Knowledge of technologies

- Knowledge of diagnostic tools and their use

- Analysis skills

Coexistence with Other Methods

Background

There are very many problem diagnosis methods, some of which at first glance seem to compete directly with RPR. However, in reality few other methods compete with RPR and most complement it.

ITIL-mentioned Methods

There are a number of methods and techniques listed in a section of the ITIL v3 Service Operations manual, although this particular section is a bit of a mixed bag.

Chronological Analysis

This is one of the simplest and best methods around. Simply work out exactly what happened in exactly what order so that the initial trigger for the problem can be found. This technique is a key component of the RPR method in that understanding the timeline of events is needed in analysing diagnostic data and presenting diagnostic proof of root cause – see *Principles* on page 28.

Pain Value Analysis

This is a technique to determine the impact of a problem based on factors such as the number of people affected, the frequency of the problem and the overall cost to the business. Pain Value Analysis is not a problem diagnosis method or technique but does provide a way to prioritise problems. Although RPR covers the prioritisation of symptoms that are thought to be related to a single problem it doesn't cover the area of prioritising multiple problems.

Kepner-Tregoe

~~Kepner-Tregoe Problem Solving and Decision Making (PSDM) is a~~ structured way to analyse a wide range of problems including IT issues. Developed in the late 50s and early 60s, KT is widely practiced in the IT community and for this reason we cover the subject further below. We will see that PSDM complements RPR and vice versa.

Brainstorming

Whilst brainstorming is widely practiced and has long been cited as an effective way of determining the cause of a problem it is of limited value when the problem is difficult or unusual. A major drawback with brainstorming is that it can repeatedly lead a team on a wild goose chase. It's a reasonable starting point for an investigation, and of course we all brainstorm at some level, but it's important to recognise that it can be slow and unreliable when investigating IT problems.

Ishikawa Diagrams

This is a technique to organise and evaluate information. It has been around for a long time and so many people will be familiar with its 'fishbone' diagrams. Although Ishikawa is not a problem diagnosis method it can be a useful tool to analyse data. RPR doesn't use this technique.

Pareto Analysis

This method is based on the analysis of the frequency of 'causes' of problems so that priority is given to detailed investigations that address those issues causing the greatest number of service disruptions. Therefore, in the main this is a method to prioritise investigation activities, although it is also used to identify failure trends and IT manufacturing faults. RPR does not address the area of identifying trends.

Kepner-Tregoe

In 1965 Charles Kepner and Benjamin Tregoe wrote *The Rational Manager: A Systematic Approach to Problem Solving and Decision Making* which describes a structured approach to dealing with problems. The approach was developed by observing how plant staff dealt with manufacturing problems and identifying the actions that made some staff more effective than others in resolving them. The Problem Solving and Decision Making (PSDM) concept has been refined but the structure has remained the same for more than 40 years.

The PSDM method covers:

- Situation Appraisal – what's happening and what should we do about it?

- Problem Analysis – what's causing the issue?

- Decision Analysis – what should we do to address the cause?

- Potential Problem Analysis – how could we prevent similar problems in the future?

As you would expect, RPR overlaps with some of the above, but mainly complements the KT method.

Situation Appraisal includes gathering information and data, and RPR complements PSDM in this area. Obviously, the analysis activity in RPR largely fulfils the needs of PSDM defined by Problem Analysis. This means that RPR provides a fast and reliable way to gather high-quality data that can be used as input into the Situation Analysis and Problem Analysis steps. This avoids the need to use pattern-based methods, the weaknesses of which we have outlined above.

What RPR doesn't offer is any advice on decision making i.e. should the problem be tackled in the first place, and once we know the root cause should we fix it. KT does provide help in this area.

Additionally, KT can drive business process improvements. For example, it may be determined that a problem is caused by a bug in a piece of software that should have been fixed during a recent maintenance upgrade. Further investigation reveals that the maintenance upgrade was not applied correctly. KT can help identify process and training improvements to avoid similar problems in the future. Again, RPR doesn't address this area.

RPR is optimised to find the technical root cause of IT problems and so offers PDSM users improvements in problem diagnosis speed and root cause reliability.

Other Methods

Three other methods worth mentioning are:

- Apollo Root Cause Analysis – a generic method that extends the concept of cause and effect

- 5-Whys – a questioning system

- TapRooT – a generic method based around a set of evaluation and analysis tools

Conclusion

RPR is quite different from the other methods described here and so tends to complement and supplement them. We wouldn't propose that anyone should replace RPR with any of these methods, but equally we wouldn't propose that anyone replace any of these methods with RPR.

RPR Concepts

Root Cause

Background

Establishing root cause is in effect RPR's *raison d'être*. ITIL v3 defines root cause in the following way:

Root Cause   The underlying or original cause of an Incident or Problem.

Whilst this may be correct it doesn't describe the criteria that identify a cause as 'the root cause' i.e. what does it look like and how do we know that we've found it?   As we will see, RPR defines strict criteria for the identification of root cause.

Technical and Non-technical Root Cause

Establishing or confirming the root cause of a problem is probably the most important Problem Management task. There are two categories of root cause; technical and non-technical.

Technical root cause includes:

- Hardware fault
- Software bug
- Misconfiguration
- Overload
- System design mistake

Non-technical root cause includes:

- Human mistake

- Lack of training

- Incorrect or weak process

- Inadequate support contract

- Inappropriate policy

For example, it may be determined that a recurring service failure is due to a software bug in a server operating system. In this case the **technical root cause** would be the software bug and the fix may be to apply a patch.

It may then be discovered that the required patch was included in a Service Pack that has been applied to the server incorrectly. The mistake was made because a poorly-trained systems engineer applied the service pack while the person who normally does the work was on holiday. To avoid future problems, the systems engineer could be retrained. Alternatively, the Change Management process could be improved so that only trained and experienced systems engineers apply Service Packs.

Reapplying the Service Pack will undoubtedly fix the immediate problem, but addressing the people and process issues will eliminate the root cause and prevent similar problems happening in the future. This is the **non-technical root cause** element.

	Technical root cause only
	RPR deals with the technical root cause of a problem only. Other complementary methods are available to deal with issues such as skills and process.

Root Cause Chain

Any problem has a chain of root causes, and so we must consider the perspective in terms of roles and responsibilities.

Imagine a simplo system that has the following major components:

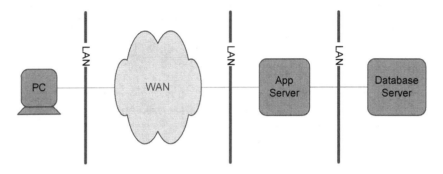

Figure 11 Root cause chain

The user experiences intermittent application errors. It's discovered that:

- The error occurs due to a problem with the Application Server – pass to Server Support

- The problem in the Application Server is with third party software – pass to the Software Supplier

- The third party software problem is due to a DCOM bug – pass to Microsoft DCOM support

- The DCOM problem is due to a Win32 API problem – pass to Windows O/S support

- The WIN32 API problem is due to an incorrect logic test in the code

NB: This scenario is entirely fictitious.

The above is a chain of root causes and the one that the Problem Solving Group needs to identify is dependent on whom they are working for. In an end-user business, the root cause identification responsibility would normally end when the third party software is proven to be the cause of the problem. At this point diagnosis responsibility would pass to the software supplier. If the Problem Solving Group is working for Windows O/S Support then root cause may not be identified until the root cause is proven to be in a particular Win32API code segment.

In summary:

One man's root cause is another man's symptom.

Pragmatic Choice of Root Cause

We will see later that RPR requires the selection of a single symptom for investigation. Sometimes a group of symptoms that are linked will be present. Perhaps the symptoms are that:

- The user tries to save a document to a network drive and the Application gives an 'Invalid Page Fault' error

- Windows Explorer shows that the network drive has become disconnected

- A network trace of the problem shows that the SMB session to the file server has failed due to excessive TCP packet loss

Through earlier analysis we might determine the following relationships:

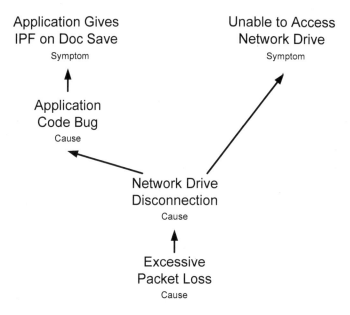

Application Gives
IPF on Doc Save
Symptom

Unable to Access
Network Drive
Symptom

Application
Code Bug
Cause

Network Drive
Disconnection
Cause

Excessive
Packet Loss
Cause

Figure 12   Cause Tree

Given this chain of causes, one could:

- Pursue the application Invalid Page Fault (IPF) – after all an application should never IPF

- Try to tune the TCP retry mechanism so that packet loss doesn't cause a Network Drive Disconnection and hence cause the bad code in the application to run

- Investigate and resolve the cause of the Excessive Packet Loss, so that the Network Drive Disconnection doesn't occur and the bad code in the application isn't run

At first glance it would be reasonable to conclude that the application IPF should be pursued, as it's possible to prove to the supplier that there is a software bug. However, getting a fix may take time and even after the fix is applied the user will still not be able to save application documents. Tuning the TCP retry mechanism will merely mask the problem. It would be best to determine the root cause of the Excessive Packet Loss.

Secondary Symptoms

A related issue is that of secondary symptoms. It might be obvious from the outset that a particular problem is only arising because a more fundamental problem exists. For example, we may run out of space on a disk volume because we fill it with log messages which are caused by a software failure. Whilst we might want to limit the log size this is a secondary symptom of the software issue. This is a rather obvious example but secondary symptoms can be far more subtle, and we have found that people may wish to focus on these if it fits with a particular agenda.

Multiple Root Causes

In an ideal world a singular problem could be tracked back to a single root cause. In the real world this is not always the case, and the tougher problems to fix are those with multiple root causes. If the possibility of multiple root causes is ignored then often the problem, and the results of any attempt to diagnose it, will not make sense.

Remote Office

Data Centre

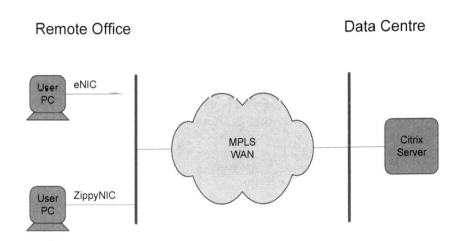

Figure 13 Problem with multiple causes

Consider the above system. User PCs are intermittently disconnected from the file server. After carrying out some investigation it's discovered that the User PC Ethernet interface goes into a 'disabled' state at the time of the problem. Upon further investigation this is found to be a known problem when eNIC cards are used in conjunction with the particular Ethernet switches used in the Branch LAN, and there is an updated driver available.

"But", says the network manager, "We get the same problem with machines with ZippyNIC cards. We don't want to update all the drivers if it is not going to fix the problem." This is a typical pattern method point of view.

Was the initial diagnosis wrong? Probably not. There is absolutely no point speculating why the ZippyNIC equipped PCs also fail. They could very well have another problem. The correct course of action is to fix the known problem and then review.

After fixing the problem with the eNIC cards it's found that both eNIC and ZippyNIC equipped PCs are suffering from server disconnects due to an excessive rate of packet loss, which is in turn due to WAN overload.

"We've looked at the overload problem and we get disconnects when the network is lightly loaded," says the network manager. Again, a pattern method point of view.

When the network load was light the problems seen were probably due to the eNIC driver problem. It's evident that the combination of two causes and imperfect input information totally destroys any pattern method approach.

You can only fix what you can see
If you have solid evidence of the root cause of a problem don't get side-tracked into Pattern Method-type debates (see Pattern Method on page 17). Such debates will often start with the words: *'But that doesn't explain why…'*

Due to the evidence-based nature of RPR, the method inherently copes with such problems. We will see later that the use of definitive diagnostics ensures that multiple root causes are easily identified.

Root Cause Identification

To resolve a user's problem, IT support people will typically review the symptoms reported and attempt to restore normal service to the user directly by:

■ Following check lists

■ Applying knowledge and experience

■ Identifying similar scenarios in a knowledgebase (such as a Known Error Database) and taking appropriate actions

If the problem caused a Major Incident, a Problem Manager may perform a Root Cause Analysis to confirm that the root cause of the problem has been addressed. In this case we would step through three status points:

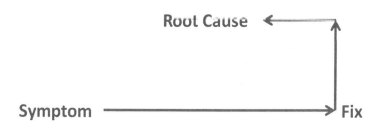

If the problem is grey, or, given the symptoms, there is no clear fix, then support staff may have to resort to trial and error to determine the fix.

The RPR approach is quite different. In common with most problem diagnosis methods, RPR starts by determining the root cause before moving on to determine a fix.

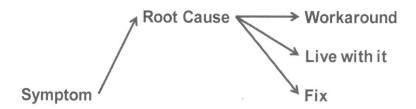

RPR refers to this scenario as Root Cause Identification (RCI) to distinguish it from the *Symptom → Fix → Root Cause* flow of typical Root Cause Analysis activity.

Once the root cause has been determined there are a range of possible responses including those shown above. Guidance on the appropriate response to a problem can be found in ITIL v3 Service Operations (section 4.4.5.8 Problem Resolution).

Symptom to Fix is Good

It's important to stress that neither this author, RPR, nor this manual is suggesting that every issue that IT support people deal with should follow the 'Symptom to Root Cause to Fix' flow. The resolution of the majority of issues would be slowed by this approach and it would obviously create a heavy support workload. If it's possible to go from Symptom to Fix with reasonable confidence that root cause has been addressed then this is the preferred route.

The point at which to switch from the standard approach to the RPR method is considered in some detail in *When to Use RPR* on page 26.

Minimum Identification Criteria

The ITIL definition of root cause is quite loose (see start of this section) which gives rise to the question, "How do I know that I have found the root cause?". RPR has a quite strict definition of root cause, as can be seen in the key point below. Such a strict definition is only possible because RPR is specific to the **technical** root causes of IT problems.

Root Cause Identification criteria
Root Cause Identification is achieved when the analysis of Definitive Diagnostic Data identifies abnormal interactions between two or more Functional Units[3], and it's possible to explain how the abnormalities cause a symptom. The Root Cause Functional Unit(s) is the one, or are those, that are acting abnormally.

Later we'll see that Definitive Diagnostic Data, Functional Units and Chosen Symptom all have a specific meaning in RPR.

---

[3] In a corporate IT support environment a Functional Unit can be thought of as a component of an end-to-end system or even as a Configuration Item (CI), and is defined on page 33.

Definitive Diagnostic Data

Possible Sources

RPR requires the capture of diagnostic data that can be directly correlated with the user's experience of the problem. The correlation is nearly always achieved by matching the time of the problem with the timings of the diagnostic events. Therefore, RPR Definitive Diagnostic Data is mostly gathered by tools that record diagnostic events with a time stamp, such as:

- Network trace

- SQL profiler trace

- PROCMON trace

- Web server log

- Syslog

- Debug log

- Custom application log

To enable statistical data (such as that produced by perfmon or sar) to be used in a similar manner, RPR provides techniques to synchronise events to statistical data entries.

Data Flows

Another way of looking at RPR is as a method to collect and use data flow information. Definitive Diagnostic Data are correlated data flows whether it be user to PC, PC to server or server to SAN.

Examples of Definitive Data

Examples of general data versus definitive data and what that data establishes are:

General Information	Definitive Diagnostic Data	Leads to statement such as…..
Observation that the web server is slow	Network analyser tracing of all traffic into and out of the web server	The network trace shows that the user's HTTP GET entered the web server at 11:50:00.690093 and the first response packet was seen at 11:50:14.324045 giving a response time of 13.633952 seconds.
Circumstantial evidence that the SQL server is slow based on test transactions	SQL Profiler Trace	The trace shows that the SQL requests associated with the slow HTTP GET all complete in a total time of less than 200ms
The Network Management System shows that the network wasn't overloaded this afternoon	Network trace on the WAN link	At the time of the problem the network was running at 85% load, most of which was due to an SMS update occurring at that time

General Information	Definitive Diagnostic Data	Leads to statement such as…..
CPU utilisation averaged over 60 seconds	CPU utilisation at 1 second intervals	At the moment the user experienced the problem the 1-second load on the application server CPU didn't exceed 42%.
Perfmon Thread object counters don't show anything unusual so it can't be an application problem	PROCMON trace	At the moment the user experienced the problem the PROCMON trace shows repeated attempts to load a particular DLL and the retries span 4.2 seconds

Even though the evidence may be buried in GBytes of data, after careful analysis it will be possible to point to one or a group of data items and state:

When the problem occurred, these diagnostic events happened

When a problem is highly intermittent, collecting such precise data is quite challenging, and significant portions of the Supporting Techniques are dedicated to this subject.

Correlation Using Markers

For information to qualify as Definitive Diagnostic Data we must be able to match diagnostic events to a user's experience of an instance of the problem (an incident). The challenge is not the generation of the data, which is relatively easy to achieve, but the ability to match the data to the incident. To help correlate diagnostic data with user incidents RPR uses a technique based on markers. By injecting markers into the diagnostic data on or around the time of the problem we can narrow the timespan we need to cover in any data analysis. Markers can be used to delimit the start and/or end of an instance of a problem to greatly reduce the work needed to analyse captured data. We cover the subject of Markers in detail on page 155.

Functional Units and Protocols

One or more components of a system can be considered as a black box provided that it has a well defined boundary or interface, and a defined set of protocols with which to send inputs, receive outputs and send control signals. If we have such a boundary we can treat those components as a functional unit.

Figure 14 The system as components

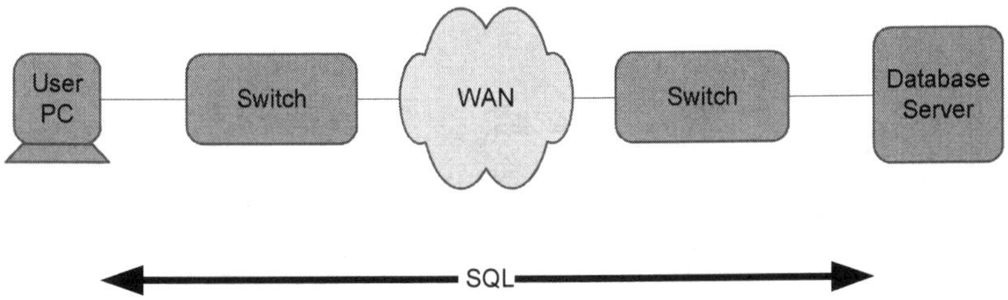

The above figure shows the flow of SQL queries and results backwards and forwards between a fat-client PC and a database server. We know that the packets in and out of the PC will contain five layers of protocol:

- SQL

- TNS – Oracle's presentation layer

- TCP – for end-to-end transport

- IP – to get the data across the network

- Ethernet – to get the data from the PC to the WAN router, and from the router to the server

Each of these protocols follows a set of rules. Knowledge of these rules provides an understanding of how the PC should interact with the rest of the system. The whole system can be treated as two functional units and provides a suitable diagnostic capture point to check the interactions between the two.

Figure 15   The system as two functional units

Functional
Unit 1

Functional
Unit 2

◀SQL▶

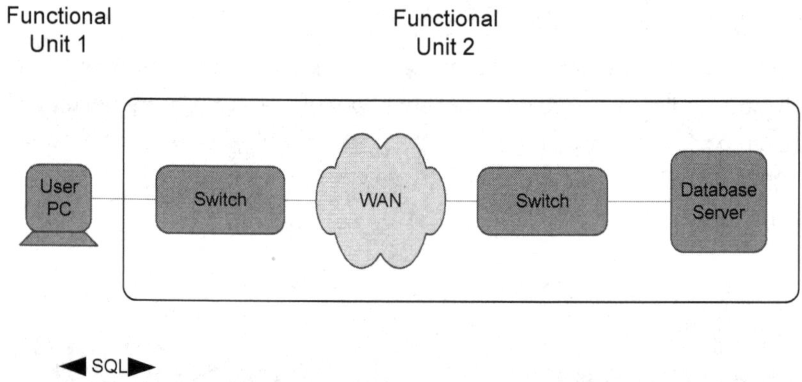

Many mainstream protocols, such as most of the TCP/IP suite, have a well defined set of rules. The rules that govern the interaction across Application Program Interfaces (APIs) are also available. Within the PC you can divide the software environment into two functional units; (1) the application and (2) the OS with (say) the Win32 API rules defining the interface between them.

Fault Domain

If we capture suitable diagnostic data from the boundaries of more than one functional unit we can establish a Fault Domain i.e. a group of system components that contains one or more problem causing components.

Figure 16 Fault domain

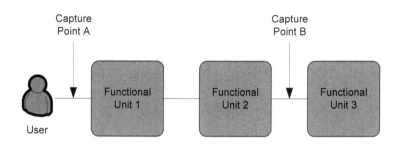

Imagine that from the analysis of data collected from the system above we find that:

■ Capture Point A data shows that requests from the user to Functional Unit 1 are good but the replies include an error, indicating a problem to the right of Capture Point A

■ Capture Point B data shows that requests from Functional Unit 2 to Functional Unit 3 are wrong, indicating a problem to the left of Capture Point B

In this case the Fault Domain is that area of the system that contains Functional Units 1 and 2[4].

---

[4] The analysis and conclusions for a system that uses a "push" model (such as price distribution) may differ a little from that shown here.

Figure 17 Narrowing the Fault Domain

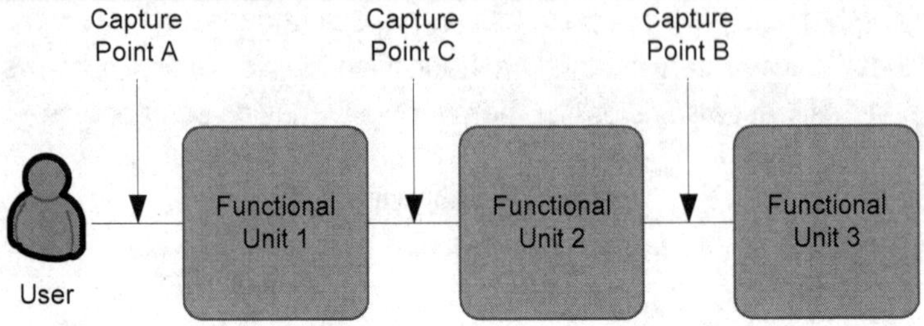

Capture Point A   Capture Point C   Capture Point B

Functional Unit 1   Functional Unit 2   Functional Unit 3

User

Adding another capture point (C) between Functional Units 1 and 2 will enable the narrowing of the Fault Domain to just Functional Unit 1 or 2.

Figure 18 Subdividing functional units

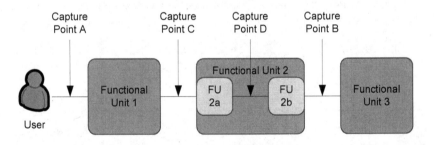

Capture Point A   Capture Point C   Capture Point D   Capture Point B

Functional Unit 2

Functional Unit 1   FU 2a   FU 2b   Functional Unit 3

User

If necessary, subdividing the functional units into smaller functional units and adding more Capture Points will allow a further narrowing of the Fault Domain.

Functional Units and CIs
In an end-user business, an RPR functional unit is analogous to an ITIL Configuration Item (CI), and in many cases there is a one to one relationship. A functional unit comprising a set of components is analogous to a Composite CI.

Network-Centric

The RPR Process and many of the Supporting Techniques can be used for all types of IT problem, and can be based around a variety of tools. Today's end-to-end systems involve a number of computers (PCs and servers) linked together by one or more data networks. Each component of an end-to-end system has an owner or technology owner, i.e. a person, who is ultimately responsible for maintaining it. Our first (and usually most important) challenge is to narrow the cause of a problem to one of these components, and so to a technology owner.

Figure 19 A network-centric system

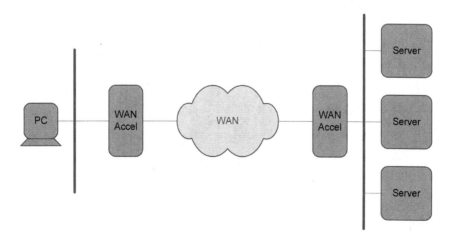

Using a Network Analyser to narrow the problem to one component has several advantages:

- Attaching an analyser to a network is non-disruptive and so can be used in a production environment

- The analyser can record every single interaction between two components

- Analysis of captures taken each side of a network gives precise details of packet loss and delay

- Analysis of captures taken in and out of a component directly identifies any misbehaviour

For this reason, the ability to use a network analyser and analyse the data it produces is an advantage. This is not as daunting as it may seem. A lot can be achieved with:

- A basic understanding of TCP/IP

- Competent use of Excel

- The guidance given in the Supporting Techniques

- Practice

Using the above system as an example, for the first pass at diagnosing a problem the chosen functional units would typically be:

- The user's PC

- The whole local LAN

- Any firewall, WAN accelerators / shapers and proxy devices

- The whole WAN

- The whole Data Centre LAN infrastructure

- Each server included in the Symptom Environment

In this case we might use multiple network analysers as shown in the following figure.

Figure 20 Placing analysers

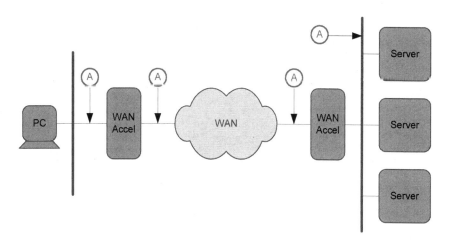

Typical Diagnostic Capture and RCI Scenario

To put the preceding information into context, and to set the scene for the RPR Core Process, it's worth outlining a typical list of actions that are used to capture the Definitive Diagnostic Data we need and the analysis of that data, which might be to:

- Set appropriate tools in place

- Relocate to a desk position near some users experiencing the problem

- Set-up / login a PC to be used to send markers

- Prepare the markers for immediate transmission (e.g. type the command but don't hit Return)

- Ask the users nearby to stop immediately they get the problem and tell you

- Activate the tools

- Wait for the problem

- Send the markers

- Confirm the users did nothing after the symptom appeared

- Take careful notes of their name, IP address, what they did leading up to the problem, etc.

- Repeat the above steps twice more to capture three examples in total

- Stop the tools

- Find the markers in the diagnostic data

- Analyse the diagnostic events immediately prior to the markers

- Identify abnormal activity

- Determine root cause

The example above is just that – an example – but it does demonstrate some of the principles of RPR.

Roles and Responsibilities

The actual allocation of roles and responsibilities will vary from business to business. There are two main roles to be fulfilled:

Problem Analyst – One person should take the technical lead for the investigation. Ideally, this would be a senior technical person who probably won't be an expert in all of the technologies involved but can communicate with Subject Matter Experts at a peer level. An external RPR practitioner can successfully fulfil this role.

Problem Manager – This role can be fulfilled by an incident, problem, recovery or service delivery manager. It's the Problem Manager's responsibility to:

- Liaise with the business

- Manage actions

- Chase suppliers

- Liaise with technical support managers to obtain resources

- Liaise with other IT groups (such as a CAB)

- Facilitate the PSG Workshop

The Problem Analyst can also take on this role but in a large organisation the job can consume a lot of time and so detract from focused investigation and diagnostic work. It's difficult for an external RPR practitioner to take on this role as the activities are mostly based on knowledge of the business structure, policies and procedures, and relationships within the business.

A suggested breakdown of responsibilities is included in Appendix D – Responsibilities on page 237.

RPR Core Process

1.01 – Understand the Problem

Purpose

End-User Symptoms

It's common to hear the complaint, "The network's slow". But what does that term actually mean? What's slow, and how slow is slow? Unfortunately many problems are investigated based on a problem description of "The network is slow".

Another typical example is:

Problem Record Description:	The users get network drive failures.
Actual Symptom:	Windows XP SP2 users try to save a Word document to the U: drive and intermittently get the message:
	'Microsoft Word has encountered an error...'

The actual symptom is very different to the problem as recorded in the Problem Record and so any diagnostic effort is likely to be poorly targeted.

The difference between the real and perceived symptoms can be quite subtle. Consider a report that users intermittently experience a delay of 30 or more seconds when trying to open a Word document from a network folder. There are at least two different ways they might open the document:

■ Within Word click on File then Open, then navigate to the network folder and double click on the document

■ Start Windows Explorer, navigate to the network folder and then double click on the document

These two scenarios are quite different from a diagnosis point of view. For example, the second scenario may require the start up of Word and perhaps the problem is in this area and not in the retrieval of the document from the network folder.

Operational Symptoms

IT operations people use systems and services, and in this way any problem they face should be treated in the same way as end-user problems outlined above. On occasions recurring issues will be detected by tools and monitoring systems that don't impact on service but do give cause for concern. A typical example is a recurring error message in a system log. In such cases the event causing concern (in this example the error message) is the symptom.

Identifying operational symptoms associated with end-user symptoms can be very useful. For example, an intermittent problem experienced by a user may have an accompanying error in a system log. It's easier for IT people to investigate the cause of the error message as the symptom is more visible to them and the symptom information will be of higher quality (time-stamped, consistent description, etc.).

In Summary

Through the execution of this step we gain a thorough understanding of the symptoms being experienced.

Objective

Following this step the problem must be understood to a level whereby the Problem Analyst could perform the actions that cause the problem. If the problem has multiple symptoms each must be understood to the same level of detail.

This does not mean that the Problem Analyst needs to recreate the problem personally or even perform the actions that cause the problem. However, this step must produce an accurate list of the keystrokes and mouse clicks that cause each symptom experienced.

The Problem Analyst must also have an accurate and detailed understanding of the exception condition, which will be either:

- One or more error messages – a record of the text verbatim

- Response time during slow performance – as well as an acceptable response time value

In the case of an operational problem, verbatim detail of error messages is the key symptom information.

Finally, the boundaries of the problem must be clearly understood; who is suffering the problem and under what circumstances (certain times of the day, certain days of the month, etc.).

Offshore call centre woes

It's astounding just how much effort an IT support operation will put into the recovery from an incident or the investigation of a problem based on the scantest of information in the Incident Record and without any further checks with the user.

Take the case of the offshore call centre that accessed systems based in the UK. Call Centre Agents complained that they experienced intermittent failures. The Service Desk categorised the repeated incidents as a network issue because UK users of the same system didn't complain and offshore users had earlier experienced some issues related to the network connecting them to the data centre. Descriptions of the problems in the Incident Record were vague, focusing on which user type, the time of day and how often. The issue quickly escalated, dragging in more and more people from service delivery, the network team, the network provider and server support. After several months the service delivery team phoned a Call Service Agent, asking them to explain the problem. The Call Service Agent described three faults, all of which were obviously application errors and unrelated to the network.

Activities

User's Perspective

It's common for an IT Support Team to begin work on a tough problem without speaking to a user, or worse still with a very vague description of the problem. This is a big mistake that leads to a misunderstanding of the problem resulting in wasted time and effort. A typical scenario is:

- The user phones the Service Desk who create an Incident Record based on the initial conversation with the user

- The Service Desk categorises the incident based on a predicted causing technology

- The Service Desk can't help and so passes the issue to 2nd Line Support

- The 2nd Line Support people start working on the incident purely based on the sketchy information received from the Service Desk

- Repeated incidents eventually result in a Problem Record with equally sketchy information

There are often inaccuracies in the information gathered by the Service Desk. Additionally, all sorts of assumptions are made without checking any of the facts, and incidents with similar symptoms may be assumed to have the same root cause.

Nothing beats a first-hand account of a problem, particularly if the user can demonstrate the problem, or at least demonstrate the scenario leading up to the problem.

There are some other aspects of dealing with end-users that you must consider:

- They have their own job to do and a problem simply prevents them from doing it. However, they are usually very willing to help.

- Everyone in business uses jargon and acronyms, not least IT people. Many users feel that this is just used to cloud an issue, or lock them out.

■ You can't expect a user to distinguish between the loss of a service due to a server failure and loss of the same service due to a router failure. There may be some subtle differences but these may not be obvious to the user. However, just because they don't understand all the ins and outs of IT doesn't mean they lack intelligence, or plain common sense.

**If you think IT is complex try talking
to a financial trader about derivatives.**

If the problem is reproducible, copy down the precise wording of any error messages that appear or, better still, have the user take a screen-shot of the message.

	Treat the category with care
	When an incident or problem is recorded in an ITSM system, it's not unusual for the associated category to be based on the predicted or perceived cause. When pursuing a problem with RPR it's important that any such categorisation is ignored.

Boundaries

To help us determine how, where and when we should gather diagnostic data we must establish the boundaries of the problem, which are:

■ Who's affected (individuals, job roles, location, PC types, etc.)?

■ When are they affected (time of the day, day of the week, day of the month, etc.)?

■ How frequently does the problem occur (twice an hour, once every two days, etc.)?

It's important to eliminate from the investigation any groups of people who may not be getting the problem. The information gathered will ultimately determine which group of users will be studied in the search for the root cause. For this reason, it is better to have an incomplete list than a list that includes people who perhaps do not experience the problem.

The time of day of the problem may relate to workload or coincide with the running of certain batch jobs. It's important to discover this information so that a plan to capture diagnostics can be set in motion at a time when the problem is typically seen.

	RPR doesn't use patterns
	Questions like "Who gets the problems and when?" are typical of a pattern-based method. **Don't be tempted to use this information** **to have a stab at guessing a common Root Cause.** It's important to remember that RPR is not a pattern-based method. The environmental questions in this step are purely to help explain the problem to others and help determine where and when and under what circumstances to investigate the problem.

Response Time Measurement

Getting a realistic idea of the magnitude of slow performance can be a little challenging, particularly if the problem is intermittent. People (this author included) are not good judges of response times. A response time of 10 seconds can easily be perceived as " ...more than 30 seconds... ". If the problem can easily be demonstrated, the response time can be measured with a watch or the second hand on the Windows Date & Time Properties clock.

It's important to get a realistic figure for a slow response. Eventually a plan will be created that captures diagnostics precisely at the time of the problem. If there's uncertainty about what represents an unacceptably slow response time there will be uncertainty in the capture plan i.e. when should the capture be stopped – following a response time of 10 seconds which seems slow (but may turn out to be normal) or a figure of more than 30 seconds which may occur very infrequently.

	No SLA
	If the acceptable response time is not defined in a formal or informal SLA a pragmatic approach is needed. Simply measure the response time for a few transactions that the user says are acceptable and then add a margin. So for example if up to 3 seconds is acceptable define more than 6 seconds as unacceptable.
	For longer running transactions a margin of, say, 10% may be more appropriate.

Remote Users

If it is not possible to meet with the users face to face, phone a user and ask them to talk you through each action leading up to the problem. Shadowing their session as they run through the steps is ideal. If this is not possible, have the remote user describe each step and ask a local member of staff to step through the actions at the same time so that you can gain a full understanding of the steps leading up to the problem.

Ignoring the user

A Problem Analyst was asked to look at a problem for a construction company. Users had reported network drive errors to the Service Desk. Second line support staff had taken a look at it and decided it was a problem with the network infrastructure. After four days of trying to track down a network infrastructure problem they called Advance7 in desperation. After an initial discussion with the Network Manager and one of his support people the Problem Analyst asked if he could meet with a user. "Why?", asked the Network Manager, "They are mostly secretaries". They reluctantly agreed.

Accompanied by the support guy, the Problem Analyst introduced himself to a lady who suffered the problem and explained why he needed her help. He asked her to describe the problem.

"Most of my work is done in WordPerfect (a word processing package). I have found that when I type a long letter I get the network message."

"Do you get the problem with any other programs you use?" the Problem Analyst asked.

"No, just WordPerfect."

It was obvious that this was a revelation to the support guy. The Problem Analyst asked the secretary to recreate the problem and sure enough after about 10 minutes of typing the network problem occurred. At the bottom of the screen was a give-away message. It said "AUTOSAVE".

Suddenly it all fell into place for the support guy. "Oh no," he said, "I've just remembered. We changed the login scripts for the secretaries and I bet the autosave area is no longer mapped to a valid network drive." He was right.

A bit of a golden oldie – whatever happened to WordPerfect? – but it perfectly illustrates the danger of not talking to the user.

Supporting Techniques

Check the RPR Practitioners forum on LinkedIn for details of Supporting Techniques for this process step.

Checklist

Before proceeding to the next step the PSG or Problem Analyst must complete the following actions:

Record a detailed list of the actions leading up to the problem such that the actions can be repeated by anyone.	
Record the details of how the result of the action differs from the desired result.	
Record full details of any error messages	
Record normal and abnormal response times.	
Determine the diagnostic boundaries for each symptom.	

Next Step

- If each symptom can be explained to a level of detail such that the Problem Analyst could walk up to a PC and attempt to recreate the problem go to *1.02 – Choose One Symptom* on page 76

- If the explanation of a symptom does not include enough detail to be able to walk up to a PC and recreate the problem scenario repeat this step

1.02 – Choose One Symptom

Purpose

A problem is often perceived to have multiple symptoms, and this forms the basis of pattern-based troubleshooting methods. When multiple symptoms exist there are three possibilities:

- All symptoms have a single root cause

- Each symptom has an individual cause

- One or more of the symptoms have multiple causes

RPR addresses these possibilities in the following ways:

- If all symptoms have the same cause, solving the root cause of one symptom will fix all of them

- Multiple symptoms with individual causes can be addressed one after the other

- A symptom with multiple causes is addressed by the root cause identification nature of RPR

It's this last point that causes many other methods to fail. For example, a pattern-based method fails completely when dealing with a problem with multiple causes. The Problem Analyst will spend much time trying unsuccessfully to determine a scenario that explains the particular symptom or combinations of symptoms.

The RPR Method dictates that if you have multiple symptoms you must prioritise them, and then attack the highest priority symptom.

This is one of the controversial areas of RPR. IT managers want all the symptoms eliminated as quickly as possible and often take some convincing that taking them one at a time is the correct and fastest way to solve problems. RPR allows a slight relaxation to this rule as explained next.

Addressing Multiple Symptoms

It is not strictly possible to address multiple symptoms at one time with RPR. There are occasions when a variety of related symptoms occur very intermittently and it would be useful to have the option of capturing any one of them. This can be accommodated within RPR subject to the following caveats:

- Once the diagnostics for one symptom have been captured all future activity must focus on this one symptom

- It's accepted that by choosing one symptom there is an immediate assumption that all symptoms have a common root cause and this may not be the case

- Any change of mind regarding the correct symptom to be pursued will require a fresh start at the first step of the process

The final caveat can be a killer. One saving grace is that stepping through the process a second time will be quicker due to the familiarity with the environment, the diagnostic capture points and the data flows.

Objective

The objective of this step is to choose one symptom that will become the focus of the diagnostic efforts. RPR cannot address multiple symptoms at one time.

Activities

Choosing a symptom to pursue is a straightforward process but must be done in a predetermined order of priority:

- If the business has a preference, deal with their choice first

- If the business has no preference chose the symptom that is causing the greatest loss of service

- If all symptoms are impacting service equally, choose the one that involves the simplest end-to-end system (simplest application or least amount of infrastructure)

Always consider the symptoms in this order.

Supporting Techniques

See *Choosing a Symptom* on page 123.

Check the RPR Practitioners forum on LinkedIn for details of additional Supporting Techniques for this process step.

Checklist

Before proceeding to the next step the PSG or Problem Analyst must complete the following actions:

Prioritise the symptoms.	
Choose one symptom.	
Agree the chosen symptom with the business.	

Next Step

- Go to *1.03 – Understand the Symptom Environment* on page 79

1.03 – Understand the Symptom Environment

Purpose

A thorough understanding of the symptom environment is needed to develop an effective Diagnostic Capture Plan (DCP). The better the quality of the information the more likely it is that effective diagnostics are gathered on the first attempt.

Although gathering accurate information is preferable all is not lost if there are imperfections. The accuracy will improve when the information gathered is shared with key support staff. Ultimately, RPR's use of definitive diagnostics means that inaccuracies in initial input information are immediately evident and so can be corrected before a second attempt at gathering diagnostic data.

Objectives

The understanding of the environment should encompass:

- Application design and technology
- Data flows
- Supporting infrastructure (including servers and databases)
- Sources of diagnostic data

The level of understanding should be to a level such that:

- The environment can be explained with a few diagrams on a whiteboard or flip chart
- It's possible to explain where diagnostic data would be captured

In this step we are only interested in facts. Opinions are worthy of note but cannot be used in developing a diagnostic plan.

Actions

In this step we need to get answers to some key questions:

What Does the Application Provide to the Business?

To put the information from this step in context it's useful to gain a general understanding of the business purpose for running the application, e.g. Outlook and Exchange to provide an email service, or Fidessa to facilitate equity trading. Such information helps gain a better understanding of the criticality and impact of a problem, and the practicalities we must consider when developing a DCP.

What is the Function of the Slow or Failing Transaction?

To help understand the data flows related to the symptom it is useful to understand what the failing or slow transaction actually does. For example, a holiday booking transaction may search one or more databases to confirm that the elements of the holiday (flight and accommodation) are still available, decrease the stock levels, execute a credit card transaction through an external service and generate confirmation documentation. Such information helps gain an understanding of the data flows.

What are the Major Components Involved?

A diagram that shows every piece of hardware and software that makes up the environment is not required. A diagram showing the major components is sufficient. At the very least the diagram must show the system divided into the Functional Units we wish to consider[5].

This will provide a view of the system with a level of detail that allows us to show the data flows and the diagnostic capture points.

How do the Major Components Interact?

A transaction causes data flows within and between components of the system. It's important to understand these flows as they dictate the diagnostic capture points and the tools we will use. For example, a booking application may use a credit card gateway to process payments, but the interaction may be via shared storage, in which case a network analyser could not be used to monitor this interaction.

---

[5] Remember that this initial set of Functional Units may be subdivided later as we 'drill down' into the system.

What Diagnostic Data is or could be Made Available?

Any type of diagnostic data may be of use but of primary interest is the type where events are time stamped; typically traces and logs.

Utilisation and queuing figures, such as those available from Windows perfmon can be used if the sample interval is reduced to a figure approaching the desired response time, say 1 second. Using marking techniques (covered later) it is possible to correlate this type of statistical data with other diagnostic data and user events.

Many types of equipment, operating systems and applications provide the ability to increase the granularity and detail of diagnostic data. Some examples are:

- Cisco IOS debug levels

- Microsoft Exchange Server 2003 Diagnostic Logs

- Microsoft Windows DNS Debug Logging

- Microsoft Windows Net Logon Debugging

There are facilities like these for many pieces of hardware and software. They are not always obvious and so some research may be needed.

Supporting Techniques

Check the RPR Practitioners forum on LinkedIn for details of Supporting Techniques for this process step.

Checklist

Before proceeding to the next step the Problem Analyst must complete the following actions:

Determine what the application, system or service provides to the business.	
Determine the function of the slow or failing transaction.	
Determine the major components involved.	
Determine how the major components interact.	
Determine the diagnostic data that is or could be made available.	

Next Step

■ Go to *1.04 – Share, Gather, Explain and Sort Information* on page 84

1.04 – Share, Gather, Explain and Sort Information

Purpose

In later steps the collection of diagnostic data will be under the control of a Diagnostic Capture Plan. Before a DCP can be formulated, detailed descriptions must be agreed for:

- The single symptom that's been chosen for investigation

- The Diagnostic Boundaries of the problem; time of day, location, PC builds, types of users, etc.

- The environment, system topology and data flows

We'll do this by sharing the information gathered to this point with the Problem Solving Group. Through challenges and discussion within the PSG the information is refined.

Objectives

The objectives of this step are to agree:

- The symptom that will be investigated

- The Diagnostic Boundaries of the problem

- The environment, system topology and data flows

Activity

This step is commonly achieved via a PSG Workshop led by a Problem Manager or a senior support person with strong meeting management skills. The Problem Solving Group comprises:

- One or more people who will take the technical lead role in the diagnosis effort

- A member from each Technical Support Team that owns equipment or software that forms the Symptom Environment (potential resolver groups)

- A member of the application support staff or developers that own the application in use

- Supplier technical support staff

If the issue is related to a Major Incident it would also be wise to include a representative from at least one of the business units affected.

	PSG Workshop Leader
	The leadership of the PSG is as much about people skills as technical knowledge. Whoever leads the PSG Workshop will need to be strong enough to resist the opinions, desires and agendas of others in the room. Technical people can often put forward a very plausible case for a theory. The workshop leader will need to resist any move to follow the theory.

The PSG Workshop can be in a room with a whiteboard or around a desk with a pad of paper, depending on the size of the group. The Problem Analyst who has conducted the initial investigation should:

- Explain the symptoms noted and highlight the chosen symptom

- Explain the boundaries of the chosen symptom

- Explain the Symptom Environment (components of the end-to-end system)

Within the PSG Workshop, through an iterative process of sharing and sorting information, gathering more, explaining what is and isn't relevant, the PSG can reach the objective of having an agreed understanding of the problem. If there are doubts about input information it will be necessary to go back to the first step and re-check the information.

Don't be surprised if the cause of the problem is determined in the workshop. Once everyone has an accurate understanding of the problem it's not unusual for them to realise the cause. However, be sure that a theory is not mistaken for a known root cause and resolution. If there's doubt it's wise to continue with the determination of the root cause, particularly if implementing the 'known resolution' will take a long time or involve significant cost.

Supporting Techniques

See *PSG Workshop* on page 126.

Check the RPR Practitioners forum on LinkedIn for details of additional Supporting Techniques for this process step.

Checklist

Before proceeding to the next step the PSG must complete the following actions:

Agree an understanding of the chosen symptom.	
Agree an understanding of the Diagnostic Boundaries.	
Agree an understanding of the Symptom Environment.	

Next Step

- If the Problem Solving Group agrees an understanding of the chosen symptom, the Diagnostic Boundaries and the symptom environment go to *2.01 – Plan the Capture of Definitive Diagnostics* on page 88.

- If a common understanding of the problem cannot be agreed return to on *1.01 – Understand the Problem* page 66 to confirm or correct the facts

It's recommended that the PSG Workshop Leader circulate the output from this step by means of a Status Report. If your organisation has a Known Error Database a record should be added at this point if one does not yet exist. Known Error and Problem Management records should be updated with the output from this step to improve the quality of the information visible to others.

2.01 – Plan the Capture of Definitive Diagnostics

Purpose

RPR requires the capture of diagnostic data where the precise instance of the problem is evident. Furthermore, it must be possible to identify the diagnostic events immediately before and after the problem occurs. To achieve these two objectives requires:

■ Selection of appropriate diagnostic tools

■ Accurate configuration of the tools

■ Time synchronisation of the tools

■ Marking of the diagnostic data so that it can be correlated with the user's experience of the problem and so that the differing diagnostic data sets can be correlated with each other.

Careful planning and execution of the Diagnostic Capture Plan will save hours in the analysis phase, and is very likely to be key to successful Root Cause Identification.

Objectives

The objectives of this step are to define a Diagnostic Objective and produce a Diagnostic Capture Plan that includes details of:

■ Areas of the IT estate that are the subject of this investigation and therefore should not be changed for the duration of the investigation

■ The actions needed to install and configure diagnostic data sources and tools

■ The actions needed to install and configure diagnostic data sources and tools specifically asked for by a supplier

■ The actions needed to install and configure a marker mechanism

■ Change Requests to enable the configuration of the required diagnostic tools and capture points

- Change Requests to enable the removal of diagnostic tools

- Security Control submissions to enable the removal and analysis of diagnostic data

- The actions needed to synchronise the clocks of the diagnostic data sources or to determine their offsets from some reference

- An Event Capture Procedure to be followed when the symptom occurs

- The actions necessary to manage tools that are capturing for prolonged periods of time (such as checking that the tools are still working, deleting unwanted data, etc.)

Activities

Diagnostic Objective

Start by agreeing the Diagnostic Objectives. Typically, these will be to prove that one or more functional units are or are not the cause of the problem.

DCP

Next determine the diagnostic data you would need to achieve the objectives. Based upon the information gathered in earlier steps, determine the diagnostic tools that will be used, their location and the location of capture points.

If this step has been re-entered after determining that the Quality of Captured Data is unacceptable, this step may simply require affirmation that the current Diagnostic Capture Plan is appropriate.

ECP

The Event Capture Procedure must cover:

- The activation of the diagnostic tools

- If possible, a capture of a working example of the problem transaction with the start and end of the transaction clearly marked using the same PC and user account on the same day

- The actions to be carried out when the problem occurs – these must be in chronological order and unambiguous[6]

- The information that should be gathered at the time of the problem and how it should be recorded

- The saving and retrieval of the diagnostic data

One or more Problem Analysts should be nominated to execute the Event Capture Procedure. For intermittent problems it may be necessary to ask a user or a colleague to carry out one or more actions in this procedure. For this reason each step of the procedure must be defined very carefully and in great detail.

	If it can go wrong it will
	If there is any ambiguity in the Event Capture Procedure one can almost guarantee that it will fail. The instructions must leave no room for error. So rather than say "Stop the trace" you need to say, "Connect to the console of the server, Click on Start, Control Panel…"

---

[6] The generation of appropriate diagnostic markers is usually critical to successful analysis and so ensure this subject is covered here.

Supporting Techniques

See:

- *Definitive Diagnostic Data Sources* on page 137.
- *Definitive Diagnostic Data Collection* on page 149.
- *Markers* on page 155.

Check the RPR Practitioners forum on LinkedIn for details of additional Supporting Techniques for this process step.

Checklist

Before proceeding to the next step the Problem Analyst must complete the following actions:

Determine the objectives of the Diagnostic Capture Plan.	
Determine the diagnostic tools to be used.	
Determine the diagnostic capture points.	
Determine the types of markers to be used, if any.	
List the expected data flows and event types for each diagnostic data source.	
Determine the change control submissions needed.	
Devise a Diagnostic Capture Plan that encompasses the above.	
Circulate the DCP and gain agreement from the Problem Solving Group.	
Confirm that the DCP will produce appropriate diagnostic data with the support staff of any supplier whose technology you suspect could be the cause of the problem.	
Notify the Change Advisory Board of the ongoing activity and argue the need to avoid changes in any areas under investigation.	
Produce an Event Capture Procedure.	
Nominate one or more people to execute the Event Capture Procedure.	

Determine the level of help needed from the technical support teams and arrange accordingly.

Next Step

- If the Diagnostic Capture Plan and its objectives are agreed by all in the Problem Solving Group (and all must buy into it), go to *2.02 – Execute the Diagnostic Capture Plan* on page 94

- If the plan is not agreed then run this step again

2.02 – Execute the Diagnostic Capture Plan

Purpose

As is the way with these things, the ease of execution is very largely down to the clarity of the Diagnostic Capture Plan. A major consideration in its execution is control. It is important that the steps in the plan are followed carefully and in a very controlled manner. This can be challenging, particularly if the problem is highly intermittent.

Objectives

The objective of this step is to execute the Diagnostic Capture Plan successfully.

Activities

Things to do

The main activities are those defined in the plan. Other key points are:

- If one or more steps of the Diagnostic Capture Planor Event Capture Procedure are to be executed by other people make sure that everyone has a copy and has been briefed on the actions – don't forget shift staff

- At the point of failure gather as much information as possible from the user regarding the actions that led up to the failure and any resulting error messages

- If possible, the Problem Analysts executing the Event Capture Procedure should be located physically close to the users affected, so that there is no delay in recognising a problem

- Typically each Problem Analyst monitors a group of users and they should explain to those users what's happening and the need for immediate notification of a problem

- Synchronise data sources

Things that go Wrong

Some things that can go wrong are:

- Procedure Quality – The Diagnostic Capture Plan or Event Capture Procedure is ambiguous and a colleague or user has interpreted one of the steps in an unexpected way

- Delayed Notification – The user agrees to call the moment the problem has occurred. When he does call we find that he has done "a few more things" since the problem

- Procedure Failure – The user agreed to send a marker immediately after the problem occurred but now can't remember if he sent it during the problem, immediately after or some time later

- User Impatience – Rather than wait for the Problem Analyst to take adequate notes the user rushes on to do more work

- Freelancing – Despite having agreed to the plan, some members of the PSG think they know what's causing the problem and so make some changes

- Pragmatism – IT management decide that rather than wait for the problem to occur again they will upgrade something

Freelancing is perhaps the biggest threat since any change that was not agreed as part of the Diagnostic Capture Plan probably invalidates not just the resulting captured data, but also the understanding of the symptom and all data captured to this point.

Change control
Don't make changes prior to the first diagnostic capture. If changes are made prior to any initial captures the whole process must start again. This is crucial since any changes made might change the initial information upon which the Diagnostic Capture Plan is based.
Resist changes to the Symptom Environment during the investigation other than those agreed as part of the investigation process. In reality, this can be difficult. If changes must be made assess their impact. If there is any possibility that the change will affect the operation of the environment then explain to senior IT management and / or the business that this will at least require a restart of the RPR process. The issue then becomes a business decision; either the change is higher priority than the resolution of the problem or it is not.

The Need for Perfection

When it comes to diagnostic data, every second counts. A one second slice of a diagnostic capture might contain 250,000 event records, and so time (chronological order and absolute) is a critical metric in RPR. Analysis is made very difficult if execution of the Diagnostic Capture Plan is not carried out in a controlled manner. Uncertainty about user actions, error messages received or the point at which markers were set will add hours, or perhaps days to the analysis effort.

	Quality warning
	You must be a perfectionist in the area of data capture. If the user fails to notify you in a timely manner, or there is uncertainty about some aspect of the execution of the plan the best thing to do is go again.
	It may be embarrassing, you may upset a few people, but you will lose all credibility if you spend five days analysing data only to confirm that you don't have what's needed.
	You must be adamant about this.

Despite reading the warning above, it's almost guaranteed that on his or her first project the Problem Analyst won't pay enough attention to this aspect of data capture. It's not until the rookie is faced with GBytes of diagnostic data and only a vague idea of where the problem occurred will he or she realise the importance of carefully marking data and accurately recording detailed information, and learn to be sufficiently emphatic in requiring compliance to the DCP.

Supporting Techniques

- *Date and Time Synchronisation* on page 153

- *Markers* on page 155

- *Managing Diagnostic Data* on page 161

- *Event Capture Procedure Issues* on page 162

Check the RPR Practitioners forum on LinkedIn for details of additional Supporting Techniques for this process step.

Checklist

Before proceeding to the next step the PSG or Problem Analyst must complete the following actions. These steps must be completed for both an End User Problem and an Operational Problem except where noted.

Assess the capacity of the diagnostic tools used.	
Agree with the Change Management function that the PSG will be notified of changes to the Symptom Environment.	
Copy the Diagnostic Capture Plan to all IT staff involved and ensure they understand it.	
Copy the Diagnostic Capture Plan to all IT shift staff and ensure they understand it.	
For End User Problems, confirm that space is available near the users with remote access to marker and capture tools.	
For End User Problems, make sure the users know what we are doing and what help we need.	
Confirm that operation staff know how to contact the Problem Analyst quickly.	
Where possible, time synchronise the diagnostic data sources.	
Activate the diagnostic data capture mechanisms.	
Run a short test to confirm that each diagnostic data source contains the expected data flows and event types.	
Run a short test, send test markers and confirm that the markers are apparent in the diagnostic data.	

Start the captures and confirm that all tools are running.	
Confirm that dates, times and other relevant information is recorded for each instance of the problem.	
Confirm that details of relevant markers have been recorded for each instance of the problem.	

Next Step

■ If the objectives have been achieved go to *2.03 – Quality Check the Captured Data on page 100*

■ If the plan is sound but a mistake was made in the execution run this step again

■ If there is a problem with the plan return to *2.01 – Plan the Capture of Definitive Diagnostics on page 88*

■ If the execution reveals a misunderstanding of the problem return to *1.04 – Share, Gather, Explain and Sort Information page 84*

2.03 – Quality Check the Captured Data

Purpose

If it appears that the Diagnostic Capture Plan has been successfully completed, technical staff may be stood down, equipment may be de-installed and a roving Problem Analyst may return to his or her own office. However, once back at the office the Problem Analyst may discover that much of the data needed is missing due to the misconfiguration of tools or a misunderstanding of the data flows.

To avoid the need to execute the entire plan again it's wise to check the quality of the captured data immediately.

Objectives

The objective of this step is to confirm that the captured diagnostic data is complete and covers the correct time period.

Activities

The best way to achieve the objectives of this step is to:

- Make a list of the data flows that you expect to see from each diagnostic source

- Note the time span that must be covered based on the occurrence of the problem, allowing plenty of time before the problem and enough time after to identify the return to normal activity

- Check that in all cases the span of the diagnostic data more than adequately covers the problem period, not forgetting to allow for any time differences between capture sources

- Check that the diagnostic data contain events for the workstations, processes or user IDs that should have been captured

- For diagnostic data showing flows from the user who experienced the problem to shared servers and services (such as those evident in a network trace) check that flows to and from the user PC can be seen

- Confirm that the markers used appear in the diagnostic data, and that it's understood when markers were sent (i.e. before, during, immediately after or sometime after the user problem)

Supporting Techniques

Check the RPR Practitioners forum on LinkedIn for details of Supporting Techniques for this process step.

Checklist

Before proceeding to the next step the Problem Analyst must complete the following actions:

Determine the time span of the problem.	
Record the time differences between the diagnostic data sources.	
Confirm that the diagnostic data encompasses the period before and immediately after the problem.	
Confirm that each set of diagnostic data contains the expected flows and event types.	
Confirm that the markers are apparent in the diagnostic data and record their relevance.	

Next Step

- If the diagnostic data quality is acceptable go to *2.05 – Analyse the Captured Data* on page 103

- If the quality of the diagnostic data is unacceptable return to *2.01 – Plan the Capture of Definitive Diagnostics* on page 88

2.05 – Analyse the Captured Data

Purpose

The purpose of this step is to study and interpret the diagnostic data. This includes the correlation of the user experience with diagnostic data events, normal or otherwise.

Although the procedure of analysing the diagnostic data should be led by the designated Problem Analyst, the analysis may require help from other members of the Problem Solving Group, other IT Support Team staff, supplier technical staff or an independent external specialist.

Objectives

The objective of this step is to produce one of the following outcomes:

- The root cause of the problem is identified and supporting evidence is available

- It's determined that the captured data does not show direct evidence of the root cause although the effect can be seen, so there is a clearer understanding of the problem and an understanding of where to look next

- It's realised that the understanding of the data flows or diagnostics was incorrect but enough is now known to formulate a better Diagnostic Capture Plan

Root Cause Identification is achieved when Definitive Diagnostic Data identifies abnormal interactions between two functional units, and it's possible to explain how the abnormality causes the Chosen Symptom.

Activities

It's wise to start with a Diagnostic Analysis Plan. This helps structure the analysis and coordinate the analysis efforts of several people (perhaps from several technical support teams). The Supporting Techniques provide guidance on the formulation of a Diagnostic Analysis Plan for a particular scenario, although there are two approaches available: Edge Inwards and Parallel Analysis.

Edge Inwards

- Establish the user transaction start and end time boundaries of the problem using the notes taken

- Start with the analysis of the diagnostic data from the capture point closest to the user

- Using the user transaction time boundaries and any markers used, determine the time boundaries in the diagnostic data

- Gain an understanding of the data flows that result from the problem transaction

- Taking each data flow at a time, look for evidence of data flow failures or excessively delayed responses

- If nothing is apparent from the previous step, compare the capture data with comparable data for a successful transaction execution if available

- If the error or slow response is present but the cause is not evident then the problem occurred after the capture point (i.e. deeper into the system and further away from the user)

- If a problem is apparent, correlate the events indicating the problem with the other diagnostic data collected to discover the Fault Domain

- Work through the above actions for each set of diagnostic data, moving one step away from the user with each iteration

- Confirm that the abnormal events would explain the transaction failure or slow response time

Parallel Analysis

When a team of Subject Matter Experts are working on the analysis a useful alternative approach is to:

■ Establish the time boundaries for the problem in each set of diagnostic data

■ Within the time boundaries, allow each SME to analyse their own set of diagnostic data (application logs, network trace, SQL traces etc.) to identify abnormal behaviour

■ Confirm that any abnormal events identified are indeed associated with the failing or slow transaction

■ Confirm that the abnormal events would explain the transaction failure or slow response time

Assessment

If the root cause is not apparent from the diagnostic data determine if:

■ The Diagnostic Capture Plan was incorrect and failed to achieve the diagnostic objective

■ The Diagnostic Capture Plan achieved the diagnostic objective and now a revised plan is needed to narrow the fault domain

■ There is an incorrect understanding of the symptom, symptom boundaries, symptom environment or the diagnostic data sources

Supporting Techniques

■ *Diagnostic Data Analysis* on page 164

■ *Milestones* on page 170

■ *Comparative Analysis* on page 172

Check the RPR Practitioners forum on LinkedIn for details of additional Supporting Techniques for this process step.

Checklist

Before proceeding to the next step the Problem Analyst must complete the following actions:

Determine the time span of the problem transaction.	
Gain an understanding of the data flows within the user transaction[7].	
Identify the diagnostic events indicating an error or delayed response.	
Correlate the remaining diagnostic data with the user transaction.	
If root cause cannot be identified determine why not.	

Next Step

- If the Root Cause of the problem is evident in the diagnostic data go to *3.01 – Translate Diagnostic Data on page 107*

- Otherwise return to *1.04 – Share, Gather, Explain and Sort Information on page 84*

---

[7] Here the term 'user transaction' is used as shorthand for the interactions seen in the diagnostic data captured closest to the user and represents the closest correlation to the user's experience

3.01 – Translate Diagnostic Data

Purpose

The diagnostic data captured may contain evidence of the root cause, however it may not be in a form readily accessible by the Technical Support Team that owns the causing technology. For example, a network trace may show a slow SQL transaction that spans tens of network packets. The packets include the Ethernet, IP, TCP and TDS headers, none of which is likely to mean anything to a Database Analyst. Through simple editing of the network trace data it is possible to strip off unnecessary headers to show the SQL Query and return code in the reply.

Objectives

The objective of this step is to translate the data into a form such that the Technical Support Team that owns the problem-causing technology can understand the diagnostic evidence that has been gathered.

Activities

The activities for this step are:

- Produce a description of the fault scenario couched in terms that are familiar to the Technical Support Team

- Produce a description in similar terms to describe how the fault scenario differs from the norm

- Strip unnecessary information from the diagnostic data and assemble it in a way that the Technical Support Team will understand

If the data flow events that are slow or in error are contained in a relatively small amount of data, the data can be directly edited to show the bare minimum needed. Sometimes it is necessary to summarise the information, particularly if the problem encompasses thousands (or millions) of diagnostic events.

Figure 21   Exchange server response times

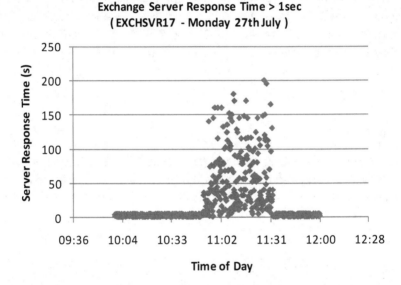

The example above was generated from network trace data. Whilst listing some of the individual transactions might be useful, listing all would plainly be impractical. The graph was produced to demonstrate the extent of the problem to the Exchange Technical Support Team.

Supporting Techniques

Check the RPR Practitioners forum on LinkedIn for details of Supporting Techniques for this process step.

Checklist

Before proceeding to the next step the Problem Analyst must complete the following actions:

Describe the problem scenario in a form familiar to the Technical Support Team.	
Produce information describing how the problem scenario differs from normal.	
Translate the evidence into a form familiar to the Technical Support Team.	

Next Step

- If the Technical Support Team confirm that they understand the translated diagnostic data and accepts that the team should take ownership of the problem, allocate the problem to the team and go to *3.03 – Work On a Fix* on page 110

- If the Technical Support Team understands the translated diagnostic data but does not accept that the problem is caused by technology that they own return to *1.04 – Share, Gather, Explain and Sort Information* on page 84

- If the Technical Support Team does not understand the diagnostic data being presented repeat this step

3.03 – Work On a Fix

Purpose

The purpose of this step is to work with the problem-owning resolver group to help them determine a fix that addresses the root cause.

Objectives

Help a resolver group determine a fix and confirm that the fix appears relevant.

Activities

The level of help that the Problem Analyst gives to the resolver group will depend on:

- KPIs
- Workload
- Particular areas of specialist knowledge
- Requirements and preferences of the Technical Support Team

As a minimum the help should include:

- Describing how the observed events vary from normal behaviour
- Answering questions regarding the capture and interpretation of the diagnostic data
- Confirmation that the determined fix seems to address the root cause

Other potential areas of help include:

- Identifying the hardware or software component that is causing the root cause

- Idontifying the configuration parameters that affect the area of operation in question

- Determining normal operation

- Helping prepare a submission to the Change Advisory Board (CAB)

Supporting Techniques

Check the RPR Practitioners forum on LinkedIn for details of Supporting Techniques for this process step.

Checklist

Before proceeding to the next step the PSG or Problem Analyst must complete the following actions:

Agree the level of help needed by the resolver group.	
Confirm that the agreed help has been provided.	
Assess the determined fix.	
Agree the planned date for application of the fix.	

Next Step

- If the Technical Support Team identifies a fix and the PSG agree that the fix addresses the root cause go to *3.04 – Implement Fix and Reactivate Capture* on page 113

- If the Technical Support Team or their suppliers cannot determine the fix from the evidence available return to *2.01 – Plan the Capture of Definitive Diagnostics* on page 88

- If there is doubt that the problem has been allocated to the correct Technical Support Team return to *1.04 – Share, Gather, Explain and Sort Information* on page 84

3.04 – Implement Fix and Reactivate Capture

Purpose

Ideally, the determined fix will indeed address the root cause. However, in some cases the fix will be applied but the users will still see the same problem symptom(s). This automatically leads to the assumption that the fix did not address the root cause. If there is only one root cause of the problem this assumption will indeed be correct.

A problem that has more than one root cause may very well display the same symptoms after the application of a fix. It is important to confirm that the fix has or has not solved the initial root cause identified, and therefore to identify any new root cause.

It's very typical for a difficult problem to be caused by more than one root cause and so this is an important step.

Objectives

Collect sufficient diagnostic data such that if the symptom persists after application of the fix, the root cause can be determined.

Activities

Standard

We must agree the criteria for determining that the fix has been effective. This will typically be a length of time without any reports of the problem. As a guideline this length of time should be twice the maximum length of time between occurrences, before the fix was applied, with a minimum of 5 working days.

The activities should be as per the most recent Diagnostic Capture Plan. With very careful consideration, it may be possible to reduce the plan by eliminating some diagnostic capture points. If in any doubt, collect all data as per the previous Diagnostic Capture Plan.

The PSG must reach an agreement with the resolver group and the business on a reasonable period for monitoring before considering the problem to be fixed.

Optional

It may be appropriate to delay the execution of this step to avoid unnecessary work if:

- The problem does not cause a major incident or significant business impact

- The problem occurs quite frequently, say once per day

- Two more occurrences of the problem would be acceptable to the business

- Appropriate resources would remain available if a second recurrence were captured

In such circumstances it might be wise to wait for one recurrence of the problem to confirm that changes have not fixed the problem before reactivating the Diagnostic Capture Plan.

Optional

The activities associated with the execution of the DCP are as described in *2.02 – Execute the Diagnostic Capture Plan* on page 94.

Supporting Techniques

- *Date and Time Synchronisation* on page 153

- *Markers* on page 155

- *Managing Diagnostic Data* on page 161

- *Event Capture Procedure Issues* on page 162

Check the RPR Practitioners forum on LinkedIn for details of additional Supporting Techniques for this process step.

Checklist

Before proceeding to the next step the PSG or Problem Analyst must complete the following actions:

Agree criteria for confirming that the fix has worked.	
Assess the capacity of the diagnostic tools used.	
Agree with the Change Management function that the PSG will be notified of changes to the Symptom Environment.	
Copy the Diagnostic Capture Plan to all IT staff involved and ensure they understand it.	
Copy the Diagnostic Capture Plan to all IT shift staff and ensure they understand it.	
For End User Problems, confirm that space is available near the users with remote access to marker and capture tools.	
For End User Problems, make sure the users know what we are doing and what help we need.	
Confirm that operation staff know how to contact the Problem Analyst quickly.	
Where possible, time synchronise the diagnostic data sources.	
Activate the diagnostic data capture mechanisms.	
Run a short test to confirm that each diagnostic data source contains the expected data flows and event types.	

Run a short test, send test markers and confirm that the markers are apparent in the diagnostic data.

Start the captures and confirm that all tools are running.

Confirm that dates, times and other relevant information is recorded for each instance of the problem.

Confirm that details of relevant markers have been recorded for each instance of the problem.

Next Step

- Go to *3.05 – Recurrence or Timeout* on page 117

	Don't be tempted to skip this step
	Even if a fix doesn't work, always confirm the original root cause still exists. A resolver group could waste a lot of time looking for an alternative fix before it's realised that what's actually needed is a fix to another root cause.

3.05 – Recurrence or Timeout

Purpose

The activities in this step depend on the success or otherwise of changes made to resolve the problem i.e. either the problem recurs or is judged as having been fixed. Partial resolution, however that may be judged, is unacceptable from an RPR process point of view and so should be viewed as a failed fix.

If the problem is unresolved then this step will produce fresh diagnostic data that can be used to confirm that the original root cause has not been addressed, or has been addressed but that another cause is evident.

It's important to note that a decision may have been made only to reactivate the Diagnostic Capture Plan if the problem recurs i.e. we will have one occurrence before reactivating the DCP – see *Activities, Optional* on page 114.

Objectives

The objectives of this step are to either;

a) confirm that any changes made have resolved the problem, OR

b) successfully execute the Event Capture Procedure if the problem reoccurs.

Any resulting diagnostic data must be at least of the same quality as was achieved during the previous capture of the problem.

Activities

The activities of this step in the case of a recurrence of the problem are identical to those of *2.02 – Execute the Diagnostic Capture Plan* on page 94.

Supporting Techniques

Check the RPR Practitioners forum on LinkedIn for details of additional Supporting Techniques for this process step.

Checklist

If the problem recurs, before proceeding to the next step the PSG or Problem Analyst must complete the following actions.

Determine the time span of the problem.	
Record the time differences between the diagnostic data sources.	
Confirm that the diagnostic data encompasses the period before and immediately after the problem.	
Confirm that each set of diagnostic data contains the expected flows and event types.	
Confirm that the markers are apparent in the diagnostic data and record their relevance.	

Next Step

- If the problem has not recurred within the agreed period for monitoring de-install tools as appropriate and exit back to the Closure Step of the Problem Management process if the ITIL Problem Management process is used

- If the chosen symptom remains go to *3.07 – Re-analyse the Captured Data* on page 121.

3.07 – Re-analyse the Captured Data

Purpose

If the problem persists despite the application of a fix, there are two explanations:

- The fix did not eliminate the root cause identified earlier
- The fix eliminated the identified root cause but there is more than one root cause

Objectives

The objectives of this step are to determine if the chosen symptom persists because:

- The applied fix did not eliminate the identified root cause, OR
- There is another additional root cause

Activities

Undertake the same activities as those described in *2.05 – Analyse the Captured Data* on page 103. Progress should be quicker due to the familiarity with the data flows and failing scenario.

Supporting Techniques

- *Diagnostic Data Analysis* on page 164
- *Milestones* on page 170
- *Comparative Analysis* on page 172

Check the RPR Practitioners forum on LinkedIn for details of additional Supporting Techniques for this process step.

Checklist

Before proceeding to the next step the Problem Analyst must complete the following actions:

Confirm that the quality of the captured data is acceptable.	
Determine the time span of the problem transaction.	
Gain an understanding of the data flows within the user transaction[8].	
Identify the diagnostic events indicating an error or delayed response.	
Correlate the remaining diagnostic data with the user transaction.	

Next Step

- If the Root Cause is the same as before return to *3.01 – Translate Diagnostic Data* on page 107

- If a new Root Cause has been identified return to *1.01 – Understand the Problem* on page 76.

The second option of returning to the start of the process may seem extreme but is needed to ensure that the symptom being experienced is indeed the same symptom. If it is, movement through the early stages of the second iteration of the process will be rapid.

---

[8] Here the term user transaction is used as shorthand for the interactions seen in the diagnostic data captured closest to the user and represents the closest correlation to the user's experience

Key Supporting Techniques

Introduction

Where the previous section describes the RPR process (what to do and when) this section outlines some of the important techniques that are used to achieve the objectives of the process steps. The techniques are intended to be very practical and therefore refer directly to technologies. Obviously information technologies are continuously evolving and Advance7 has a continuous R&D programme to develop techniques to keep pace with the changing environment. Although the latest techniques can be found on the RPRsupport.com website, there are sufficient techniques in this section to enable the RPR practitioner to investigate any problem to a considerable depth.

Choosing a Symptom

When faced with multiple symptoms it can be difficult to choose one to pursue. This section provides some guidelines to help the PSG identify the highest priority issue.

A single problem may be visible as multiple symptoms, and may cause secondary problems. The RPR method dictates that we should investigate specific incidents of a single symptom. Therefore we must prioritise the symptoms and then focus on the highest priority one. The explanation is:

**"If we fix this problem and it fixes all the others – great.
If not, we'll move to the next on the list."**

It's important not to try to deal with multiple symptoms as this leads immediately into a pattern-based approach and is the most common reason for failure of previous attempts at diagnosis.

Your Preferred Symptom

To simplify problem diagnosis, the preferred symptom will be the one that involves the least amount of equipment and software, or the simplest technology. Here are a couple of examples:

Users complain that Excel hangs when manipulating a complex spreadsheet which has links to many workbooks stored on network drives. However, the problem can be recreated with a large but simple spreadsheet saved on the local disk. The preferred symptom is that of the second scenario since it avoids the complexity of workbook links and the use of a network drive.

Remote users of an insurance actuarial system complain that it occasionally hangs. Remote users access the system via Citrix. However, users at Head Office use a fat client version of the system and get the same problems. Unless there is a compelling reason to deal with the remote users (and there can be political and other reasons) recommend that the fat-client system problem is investigated first. This would avoid the added complexities of the WAN and the Citrix environment.

	Be sure of the symptoms
	It's critical that the symptom of a simpler scenario is identical to that of the more complex one. Taking the Excel example above, much time could be spent fixing the simpler scenario only to find that the problem with the complex spreadsheet remains.

Business Impact

Whilst a Problem Analyst might prefer to investigate a particular symptom the overriding factor will be what the business considers to be the highest priority issue and this won't always be obvious from an IT point of view. The Problem Manager should ensure that he or she thoroughly understands how each symptom impacts the business and the perceived priority of each issue.

The danger is that the PSG spends days or weeks fixing a problem it believed to be critical only to find that the business considers it trivial.

Symptoms and Politics

There can be pressure to pursue a secondary symptom (see *Secondary Symptoms* on page 48) for no logical reason. A similarly baffling situation can arise when one or more people don't want a problem fixed. Typical reasons are:

- Contractors believe that their repeated involvement in the recovery from an Incident is guaranteeing their tenure

- Staff receive significant overtime payment for repeatedly dealing with a recurring Incident

- The justification for an upgrade is in some part based upon the proposition that it will resolve the problem

- A member of staff wants to include a technology on their CV and has justified its purchase based on the proposition that it will resolve the problem

In these cases the PSG should cease all work on the problem and handle as local rules and customs dictate.

That's not the answer wanted

We were asked by a Network Manager to prove that a client/server application was 'a load of rubbish' because it gave a nonsense message when the client intermittently lost sessions with the server. The network and applications environments were managed by two different groups of people, and they were prone to warring with each other. We weren't very popular when we proved that the problem was due to a router dropping packets. True, the message given to the user was not very informative, but the root cause was excessive packet loss.

PSG Workshop

The PSG Workshop provides an opportunity to pull the group together into a focused team. This section provides the workshop chairperson and Lead Problem Analyst with guidance in the running of the workshop.

Purpose and Objectives

A PSG Workshop is a gathering of all those members of the Problem Solving Group, optionally with the inclusion of representatives from the business, and is typically led by a Problem Manager or senior technical person. The need for a formal PSG Workshop is a matter of judgement. If the investigation is into a minor problem a simple gathering of a small Problem Solving Group around a desk may be sufficient. On the other hand, problems can escalate quickly. Disputes with suppliers or user groups can rapidly become very political and therefore each case must be judged on its own merit. Some situations where a formal PSG Workshop is preferable are:

- The problem is high profile within the IT department, i.e. the top person in IT is monitoring the situation

■ Board-level staff are involved

■ The IT department has become frustrated with the attempts of a supplier to fix the problem and has lost faith in them

■ There is a dispute within the IT department

■ There is a dispute between the IT department and a supplier

■ There is a dispute between suppliers

The objectives of the PSG Workshop are:

■ Credibility – For the Problem Analyst to establish his or her credibility so that the group will accept opinion and guidance

■ Rapport – To build rapport and a team spirit within the Problem Solving Group quickly – fixing a problem whilst battling against staff, colleagues or suppliers is extremely difficult

■ Calm – To make peace between members of the Problem Solving Group – co-operation between all involved will greatly help

■ Share, Gather, Explain and Sort

  ● Share the information known at this point with the Problem Solving Group

  ● Gather further facts but mask out opinions

  ● Correct any misunderstandings regarding the problem, the technologies involved or the supporting infrastructure

  ● Sort the facts into Symptoms, Boundaries and Other Observations

■ Agree an Understanding of the Problem – It is essential that everyone in the PSG shares a common understanding of the problem before determining the next step

■ Agree on Action – The PSG must agree a Diagnostic Objective and detail a Diagnostic Capture Plan to achieve that objective.

Take control
The PSG may include people who don't know, understand or believe in RPR. Initially you should try to sell the concept to them but they may try to railroad the discussions in a certain direction. Ultimately the Problem Analyst must wrestle control from these people.

Establishing Credibility

To establish credibility, at the first meeting of the Problem Solving Group the Problem Manager should explain her role and that of the Problem Analyst. Making it clear that the sole objective is to find the cause of the problem should help dispel fears that there may be a hidden agenda.

Where the Problem Manager is not known to everyone in the meeting, a brief explanation of his or her background will help establish credibility. A number of the attendees will immediately relate to the Problem Manager just because they share a similar background.

Building Rapport

To build rapport with those at the meeting the chair should ask them to introduce themselves to the others and to explain their relationship to the problem. As they introduce themselves try to make out a seating plan of those around the table. This will help you recall at a later stage who's who. If you don't fully understand their role, probe a bit further. Asking someone to talk about themselves demonstrates an interest in them and helps the PSG understand the skills that are available within the group.

	Make a seating plan
	Draw a rough plan in your notebook showing where each person is sitting and make a quick note of their job function. This will help you recall who said what, and who's who long after the meeting.

This is particularly useful for the Lead Problem Analyst as a quick glance at the seating plan also enables her to address someone directly by name, which again helps to build rapport.

In a large meeting it's useful to draw the seating plan on a whiteboard for the benefit of the others in the room. It probably comes as no surprise that in a large organisation people in one part of an IT department may not know the people in another.

Calming Troubled Waters

A Problem Analyst is often dropped into very tense situations. It's not unusual to have to deal with angry people. The anger is often directed at a supplier, a member of the support staff or even the Problem Analyst. There can be similar feeling in the other direction. There is one golden rule here for the Problem Analyst:

Don't take sides or make a snap judgement

The Problem Analyst must be very careful not even to hint at some pre-judgement.

Brought to account

Some time ago, an Advance7 Problem Analyst went to look at a problem for a large accountancy practice in the Midlands. He arrived at their plush offices and was quickly greeted by the Network Manager who said, "Thank God you're here, they're all waiting for you." Not certain what this meant, the Problem Analyst was led to the boardroom from where raised voices could be heard. There, waiting for him, were three IT staff, a senior partner of the practice and representatives from two suppliers.

A supplier gave him a brief résumé of the problem. Users were intermittently losing their connection with the main fileserver. From the description of their diagnostic findings, it seemed like a server problem. The senior partner said that the Problem Analyst had been asked to attend to confirm that the present problems with their network were all down to the servers.

"Do you agree, it must be the server?"

Just as well the Problem Analyst remained impartial – it turned out to be a cabling problem.

It's a good idea to just listen to each side's complaints and let them blow themselves out, but do this prior to the meeting if possible. If bad feeling between groups is dealt with in the meeting there will be things said that will be rash and difficult to retract. This will cause a bigger problem in building a working relationship between all groups.

Without some exploratory discussion beforehand, there will be people in the meeting who are carrying a great deal of anger with them and will not be ready to tackle the problem in an objective way. Even if someone in the meeting has unreasonable gripes, try to find a valid point, and reflect that back to them.

"So Karen, can I just get this straight? This is giving you problems with completing order processing on-time and impacting the morale of your staff."

More than just listening to complaints, it's necessary to demonstrate an understanding of the issue. At the end of the outpouring Karen will feel that she has said her piece, and won't need to raise the same points again. Be careful not to let her go off at a tangent though.

If your angry person does go off at a tangent and start complaining about, say, the company's server strategy set this concern aside by:

■ Being seen to be making a note of the concern

■ Telling the complainant that this issue is outside the remit of the PSG

■ Agreeing to note it as a point of concern in the final report

This should help produce a more positive approach to the problem in hand.

Information Sorting

Write three headings on a whiteboard or flipchart:

■ Symptoms – Under this heading write one line descriptions of the symptoms

■ Diagnostic Boundaries – Under this heading note the when, where and in what circumstances information that will affect the Diagnostic Capture Plan

■ Other Observations – Here note information that may or may not be related to the problem

Summarise the information gathered to this point and sort it amongst the three headings. This should be done in front of the Problem Solving Group to allow others to question and correct the facts.

Don't mix symptoms with other stuff
Don't mix boundaries, other observations, concerns or theories in with the symptoms of the problem. This is a common area of confusion for new RPR practitioners.
If the piece of information includes actions that would enable someone to attempt to recreate the problem it's a symptom. In all other cases it's not a symptom.

Ask each person who has been directly involved in the investigation what action they have taken and what they have found. As you gather more information sort it:

- Is it relevant?

- Into which section of your whiteboard does it fit; Symptoms, Diagnostic, Boundary or Other Observation?

Some issues must be set aside. Some of the information gathered will be opinions and or commentary on strategic issues.

**"I reckon it's the server – we've had
loads of problems with those HP boxes."**

**"I don't know why we installed Cisco anyway.
We should have gone for Juniper."**

These comments may be expressed as possible causes of the problems and it's important that they are not dismissed in an off-hand manner. What's being said may be totally incorrect but the Problem Manager needs to avoid alienating anyone in the group. Ask for the reasoning for their view. They may then convince themselves that they are wrong, or it may be possible to explain any incorrect deductions. If the view is wrong it's preferable to explain why otherwise the proponent will get stuck on this one idea, and this will prevent him or her from considering alternatives. Of course, he or she may convince the group that they are correct, or at least that there's an important area that has not been considered.

Educating along the way

We went to a site where PCs were losing connections with a server. Prior to attending the initial meeting we had seen network management statistics showing a high rate of port errors. The IT staff told us that they were convinced that these errors were being caused by an upgrade of the server software.

We explained the basic operation of the network and the meaning of the errors. Those present quickly accepted that server software was unlikely to be a cause of the errors. Of course that did not mean that server software could not be a cause of the disconnects.

It's important to separate symptoms from other information as there is a great danger that the group will get side-tracked and treat a general observation or opinion as if it was a symptom or possible cause.

Agree an Understanding of the Problem

It's during the PSG Workshop that a commonly agreed understanding of the symptoms is achieved in terms of:

- Symptom description
- Symptom environment
- Symptom boundaries

If multiple symptoms are present, the PSG should agree the priority of each and hence determine which symptom will be investigated first.

Agree the Diagnostic Objective and Capture Plan

Once the information has been sorted into symptoms, boundaries and other observations, add two further headings:

- Possible Causes – Under this heading list the functional units that make up the end-to-end system

- Diagnostic Objective and Capture Plan – Here note the objectives of the Diagnostic Capture Plan and the tasks to achieve those objectives.

Using the agreed understanding of the symptom environment, the PSG should next list the functional units that could cause the problem. It's important not to describe detailed theories of the cause, but to simply list the functional units in the end-to-end system.

From the list of possible causes the PSG should agree a Diagnostic Objective which will typically be based on proving that a functional unit is or is not the cause of the problem. In the formulation of the Diagnostic Capture Plan the PSG must be certain that:

- Adequate and suitable diagnostics can be gathered from the functional unit boundaries

- Necessary tools are available

- Important data flows will be captured

■ It will be possible to correlate data flow events with the user's experience of the chosen symptom

It's easier to deal with a few large functional units than many smaller ones. If the problem happens quite frequently, keep the functional units quite large (PC, Network and Server). If it will be difficult to capture Definitive Diagnostic Data, make the functional units more granular (PC, Edge Switch, Core Switch, Router).

	Techie love
	Although all new Problem Analysts joining Advance7 undergo extensive RPR training we often hit the same problem. Technical people are very keen on the techie aspects of RPR, and so dive headlong into gathering and analysing diagnostic data. Unfortunately they sometimes forget to define a Diagnostic Objective and so have no idea what they are trying to achieve with the analysis. **Make sure the Diagnostic Objectives have been clearly defined.**

Closing

At the close of the meeting:

■ Ask for everyone to confirm that they agree with the objectives of the Diagnostic Capture Plan

■ Ask if anyone can see a problem with the execution of the plan

■ If possible, agree a date and time for an update meeting

Factional fighting

Whilst dealing with a network problem, a Problem Analyst found entrenched hostilities between two groups within the IT department. One group controlled and supported a number of remote UNIX systems, whilst the other was responsible for the private network used to link the remote systems into the Head Office. The analyst suspected a mismatch of UNIX and network parameter settings and suggested to the system guy that they meet with a network analyst to discuss the problem.

"I'm sorry, I don't have time."

The Problem Analyst tried pushing the point only to be told:

"I don't see why I should meet with him,
I thought that's what you guys are here for."

He then made some rather derogatory remark about his 'colleague' and walked away.

Luckily, although the network analyst didn't like the systems guy he was a little more reasonable and agreed to come with the Problem Analyst to talk to him. The cause of the problem was determined within about 10 minutes.

Definitive Diagnostic Data Sources

An essential aspect of designing a Diagnostic Capture Plan is understanding the DDD sources available. Here we outline a few common sources to help the PSG with the Diagnostic Capture Plan.

Introduction

Prior to working on a Diagnostic Capture Plan it is very useful to understand the diagnostic facilities that are available in the equipment and software that make up the Symptom Environment. Of particular interest are facilities that generate a record of timestamped events.

Web research is a good way to determine the tools that are available. Even though a tool is freely available don't assume that it is installed on the equipment within the Symptom Environment. If there is an early indication that a particular tool will be needed ensure that it is installed or determine how it would be obtained and installed.

There are so many tools available the choice can be bewildering. A simple and powerful tool to use as part of an early Diagnostic Capture Plan is the network analyser because:

- Its use is non-disruptive and non-intrusive (you don't have to load software onto servers, etc.)

- It can be used to prove or disprove quickly whether the problem is caused by 'the network' – which is often blamed when a grey problem occurs

- You can narrow the Fault Domain to a 'box' using a network analyser, and this usually means that you can identify the owner of the technology causing the problem

- Traces of interactions with a 'box' will often give a very big clue as to the problem within it

- Network traces can provide hard evidence that can be passed to a supplier

If you narrow the problem down to a server but are unable to determine what component is the root cause, you'll need to drill down further. The ways to achieve this in order of preference are:

■ Turn on additional system and application debug capabilities

■ Ask the developer to add some simple instrumentation (unfortunately rarely acceptable)

■ Use specialist tools such as Process Monitor and Xperf in a Windows environment or strace for UNIX problems

	Expert tool warning
	Expert tools make mistakes. You need to understand the basis on which they are identifying problems i.e. you need to understand the technology being analysed, and you need to consider the environment in which the tool is running.

Beware of anyone who tries to sell you an 'expert tool' with the claim that you don't need to know anything about the technology to use the tool. This is a complete falsehood. 'Expert tools' make glaring mistakes, and unfortunately an operator who doesn't understand the tool's underlying principles will trust it without questioning. This leads to much wasted time. The benefit of an 'expert tool' is that it can provide a short-cut to a problem cause. As long as you can distinguish between an incorrect interpretation of data and a real problem, an 'expert tool' can speed up fault diagnosis.

Not so expert

A Problem Analyst was working with a group of network engineers from a supplier to find the cause of a server disconnection problem. The engineers had connected an expensive analyser to the network running in Expert Mode and the problem Analyst was using the freely available Wireshark in another part of the office.

After about twenty minutes one of the engineers came racing round to tell the Problem Analyst proudly that he had found the problem and it was a WINS failure. This seemed strange as the servers concerned were NetWare, but the Problem Analyst went along with him to view the trace.

Sure enough, the expensive analyser claimed that there were serious WINS problems – WINS names resolution requests were not being answered by the WINS server. The Problem Analyst asked to view the trace in 'Non-expert Mode'. It showed lots of PCs sending out WINS requests but no responses. However, what the analyser didn't realise (and how could it) was that it was sitting on a switch. The WINS requests were sent broadcast so would be seen by the analyser, whereas the WINS reply would be sent unicast and would not be seen.

This illustrates a big problem with 'expert tools' – they do not and cannot take into account the environment in which they are running.

The Network Analyser

Network analysers used to be very expensive – Advance7 bought one in 1990 that cost £32,000. Those days are long gone. Network analyser software is now available for any laptop.

Network analyser costs

You will get 85% of all the functionality you will need from a free tool. You'll get another 10% from a top-of-the-range tool. So you just need to decide if the extra 10% is worth the price tag.

There will be 5% of functionality that you can't get from either.

Certainly for the newcomer to network analysis, we recommend Wireshark which is an extremely powerful and robust tool and completely free. If your needs are more sophisticated or the culture of your company is such that you need to buy a commercial product make your selection with your eyes wide open by gaining experience with a free or low cost tool first. Once you understand its shortcomings you'll be in a good position to buy something more powerful.

Don't buy into the concept that an analyser can be used for BOTH monitoring AND troubleshooting. Monitoring tools are great for the job intended but often have limitations such as capture buffer size and few protocol decodes that make them less than ideal for troubleshooting. Aside from this, it's unrealistic to think that you will be able to stop ongoing monitoring and refocus a tool while you troubleshoot a problem.

Prior to making your purchasing decision, always ask the supplier for a loan or hire unit and test the facilities that are important to you. Marketing material often overstates a product's capabilities and the devil is definitely in the detail.

Performance Probes

A number of companies market hardware probes or server agents to diagnose performance problems. The probes monitor network traffic and perform deep packet decoding to work out the time difference between a service request and the corresponding response. This can greatly speed up the diagnosis of problems but it is important that you understand the limitations.

In a multi-tiered environment, these probes will treat each tier in isolation. Although the probe management system will attempt to show an end-to-end view of performance, this is done on a statistical basis. The probes are not able to correlate an individual user request with all the data flows that result[9]. That means that if the problem is due to, say, one slow database call, a performance probe will get you to the problem quickly. However, if the problem is due to a high number of calls that execute quite quickly the performance probe probably won't help.

Process Monitor

Process Monitor (procmon) is a terrifically powerful tool for Microsoft Windows workstations and servers. It traces and timestamps file system, registry, process activity and thread activity. Procmon timestamps have a granularity of 100ns and each trace entry includes execution duration.

---

[9] If you ask the suppliers of these probes if their product can breakdown a transaction response time into its component parts they will nearly all say yes. If you ask them to confirm that this breakdown truly correlates a user-generated event with all of the consequential service calls, many will still say yes. In fact there are only a few products that can correlate data flows through all tiers of a multi-tier system and then only for a limited set of applications.

File   Edit   Event   Filter   Tools   Options   Help

Sequ..	Time of Day	Process Name	PID	Operation	Path	Result	Detail	Duration
2393088	14:00:04.4655208	sqlservr.exe	1176	WriteFile	J:\mssql2000\mssql\data\DBA_admin_Log.LDF	SUCCESS	Offset: 7,389,184, ...	0.0003317
2393089	14:00:04.4885581	sqlservr.exe	1176	WriteFile	J:\mssql2000\mssql\data\DBA_admin_Log.LDF	SUCCESS	Offset: 7,389,696, ...	0.0003072
2393090	14:00:04.5093629	sqlservr.exe	1176	WriteFile	J:\mssql2000\mssql\data\DBA_admin_Log.LDF	SUCCESS	Offset: 7,390,208, ...	0.0003059
2393091	14:00:04.5304492	sqlservr.exe	1176	WriteFile	J:\mssql2000\mssql\data\DBA_admin_Log.LDF	SUCCESS	Offset: 7,390,720, ...	0.0002541
2393134	14:00:04.5513690	sqlservr.exe	1176	WriteFile	J:\mssql2000\mssql\data\DBA_admin_Log.LDF	SUCCESS	Offset: 7,391,232, ...	0.0002691
2393135	14:00:04.5726354	sqlservr.exe	1176	WriteFile	J:\mssql2000\mssql\data\DBA_admin_Log.LDF	SUCCESS	Offset: 7,391,744, ...	0.0002822
2393136	14:00:04.5935869	sqlservr.exe	1176	WriteFile	J:\mssql2000\mssql\data\DBA_admin_Log.LDF	SUCCESS	Offset: 7,392,256, ...	0.0002803
2393137	14:00:04.6207958	sqlservr.exe	1176	WriteFile	J:\mssql2000\mssql\data\DBA_admin_Log.LDF	SUCCESS	Offset: 7,392,768, ...	0.0002600
2393138	14:00:04.6412622	sqlservr.exe	1176	WriteFile	J:\mssql2000\mssql\data\DBA_admin_Log.LDF	SUCCESS	Offset: 7,393,280, ...	0.0003775
2393139	14:00:04.6417614	sqlservr.exe	1176	WriteFile	J:\mssql2000\mssql\data\DBA_admin_Log.LDF	SUCCESS	Offset: 7,393,792, ...	0.0006893
2393140	14:00:04.6640724	sqlservr.exe	1176	WriteFile	J:\mssql2000\mssql\data\DBA_admin_Log.LDF	SUCCESS	Offset: 7,394,304, ...	0.0002470
2393964	14:00:07.0167490	sqlservr.exe	1176	WriteFile	J:\mssql2000\mssql\data\DBA_admin_Log.LDF	SUCCESS	Offset: 7,394,816, ...	0.0003112
2426221	14:00:33.0183056	sqlservr.exe	1176	WriteFile	J:\mssql2000\mssql\data\DBA_admin_Log.LDF	SUCCESS	Offset: 7,395,328, ...	0.0005251
2426271	14:00:33.0192664	sqlservr.exe	1176	WriteFile	J:\mssql2000\mssql\data\DBA_admin_Log.LDF	SUCCESS	Offset: 7,395,840, ...	0.0005147
2427917	14:00:33.0473544	sqlservr.exe	1176	WriteFile	J:\mssql2000\mssql\data\DBA_admin_Log.LDF	SUCCESS	Offset: 7,396,352, ...	0.0004802
2428083	14:00:33.0498054	sqlservr.exe	1176	WriteFile	J:\mssql2000\mssql\data\DBA_admin_Log.LDF	SUCCESS	Offset: 7,396,864, ...	0.0004799
3758736	14:06:04.0968941	System	4	WriteFile	D:\shared\194.mark	SUCCESS	Offset: 0, Length: ...	0.0000531
3759059	14:06:04.2864453	System	4	WriteFile	D:\shared\194.mark	SUCCESS	Offset: 0, Length: ...	0.0000263
3765986	14:06:04.7293427	sqlservr.exe	1176	WriteFile	J:\mssql2000\mssql\data\Equity_Report_log.ldf	SUCCESS	Offset: 18,140,804...	0.0005801
3765998	14:06:04.7299978	sqlservr.exe	1176	WriteFile	J:\mssql2000\mssql\data\Equity_Report_log.ldf	SUCCESS	Offset: 18,140,808...	0.0003815
3766007	14:06:04.7304249	sqlservr.exe	1176	WriteFile	J:\mssql2000\mssql\data\Equity_Report_log.ldf	SUCCESS	Offset: 18,140,809...	0.0002523
3786016	14:06:07.0053108	sqlservr.exe	1176	WriteFile	J:\mssql2000\mssql\data\Equity_Report_log.ldf	SUCCESS	Offset: 18,140,810...	0.0007853
3786948	14:06:08.4954785	sqlservr.exe	1176	WriteFile	J:\mssql2000\mssql\data\Equity_Report_log.ldf	SUCCESS	Offset: 18,140,810...	0.0009019
3786949	14:06:08.4964429	sqlservr.exe	1176	WriteFile	J:\mssql2000\mssql\data\Equity_Report_log.ldf	SUCCESS	Offset: 18,140,811...	0.0002955
3945347	14:07:03.2464370	sqlservr.exe	1176	WriteFile	J:\mssql2000\mssql\data\Equity_Report_log.ldf	SUCCESS	Offset: 18,140,811...	0.0019178
3945348	14:07:03.2484289	sqlservr.exe	1176	WriteFile	J:\mssql2000\mssql\data\Equity_Report_log.ldf	SUCCESS	Offset: 18,140,813...	0.0003558
3983272	14:07:12.9518764	System	4	WriteFile	D:\shared\195.mark	SUCCESS	Offset: 0, Length: ...	0.0000643
3993529	14:07:13.2843265	System	4	WriteFile	D:\shared\195.mark	SUCCESS	Offset: 0, Length: ...	0.0000539
4119553	14:07:38.3922179	System	4	WriteFile	D:\shared\196.mark	SUCCESS	Offset: 0, Length: ...	0.0000676
4119680	14:07:39.2834478	System	4	WriteFile	D:\shared\196.mark	SUCCESS	Offset: 0, Length: ...	0.0000419
4126212	14:07:42.0023087	sqlservr.exe	1176	WriteFile	J:\mssql2000\mssql\data\Equity_Report_log.ldf	SUCCESS	Offset: 18,140,813...	0.0004967
4154509	14:07:53.7528872	sqlservr.exe	1176	WriteFile	J:\mssql2000\mssql\data\Equity_Report_log.ldf	SUCCESS	Offset: 18,140,814...	0.0004501
4154510	14:07:53.7534345	sqlservr.exe	1176	WriteFile	J:\mssql2000\mssql\data\Equity_Report_log.ldf	SUCCESS	Offset: 18,140,815...	0.0004495
4427799	14:09:02.9752885	System	4	WriteFile	D:\shared\197.mark	SUCCESS	Offset: 0, Length: ...	0.0000651
4433636	14:09:04.2807890	System	4	WriteFile	D:\shared\197.mark	SUCCESS	Offset: 0, Length: ...	0.0000380
4702968	14:10:01.8182781	System	4	WriteFile	D:\shared\198.mark	SUCCESS	Offset: 0, Length: ...	0.0000588
4705787	14:10:03.4529577	sqlservr.exe	1176	WriteFile	J:\mssql2000\mssql\data\Equity_Report_log.ldf	SUCCESS	Offset: 18,140,815...	0.0005473
4705788	14:10:03.4535899	sqlservr.exe	1176	WriteFile	J:\mssql2000\mssql\data\Equity_Report_log.ldf	SUCCESS	Offset: 18,140,816...	0.0005582
4705799	14:10:03.4543329		1176	WriteFile	J:\mssql2000\mssql\data\Equity_Report_log.ldf	SUCCESS	Offset: 18,140,817...	0.0003161

Figure 22 Procmon example

The example above shows a trace taken during the investigation of an application performance problem. A key database and its log files were located on a SAN and there was a suspicion that the SAN was causing the slow performance. Our markers to delimit transactions can be clearly seen (e.g. D:\shared\194.mark). The marker entries appear twice since these operations used a lazy writing method.

Perfmon

Use

The most common use for Perfmon (Performance in XP – Reliability and Performance Monitor in Vista) is to check the load on a server at the time of a problem.

Collection

The first thing to consider is the Sample Interval. To create definitive diagnostics from Perfmon the Sample Interval should be set to 1 second to avoid losing detail in the averaging process.

The counters collected will depend on the objective of your DCP but to obtain an indication of a resource shortage in a server or client PC the following metrics provide a good starting point:

- \\Processor(*)*

- \\PhysicalDisk(*)*

- \\Memory*

- \\NetworkInterface(*)*

where (*)* means all Instances and all Counters.

Correlation

The following correlation can be achieved:

- Perfmon to Network Trace – Include the Received Echo/sec counter of the ICMP object in the Perfmon study and send a ping as a marker. The ICMP Echo Request will appear in the network trace and the Perfmon stats.

- Perfmon to Microsoft SQL Profiler – the Client Process ID appears in the Profiler entries and in Process objects in Perfmon running on the client machine.

Some servers may be ping'd almost constantly as part of a monitoring system. If this is the case construct a batch file that sends, say, 10 pings in quick succession. The spike in pings will be visible in the Perfmon stats. This can be done as follows:

Windows batch file:
```
start ping 192.168.1.1 -n 1
start ping 192.168.1.1 -n 1
start ping 192.168.1.1 -n 1
start ping 192.168.1.1 -n 1
start ping 192.168.1.1 -n 1
start ping 192.168.1.1 -n 1
start ping 192.168.1.1 -n 1
start ping 192.168.1.1 -n 1
start ping 192.168.1.1 -n 1
start ping 192.168.1.1 -n 1
```

LINUX:
```
ping -i -c 10 0.05 192.168.1.200
```

When analysing the diagnostic data collected to investigate a performance problem the typical order of work would be:

1. Use standard RPR techniques to identify the server causing the delay, usually based on network tracing

2. Determine the precise time frame of the delay based on network trace timestamps

3. Using the ping markers that correlate the network trace to the Perfmon stats, determine the precise time frame of the delay in the Perfmon data

4. Study the server load within this time frame

Microsoft SQL Profiler

Overview

SQL Profiler can be run locally on the SQL server or remotely from a client PC. It can capture to memory or disk, and supports file rollover (e.g. 50MB max size) and trace stop time. Do not use the option to save to a database table – it is a lot slower.

Uses

The most common use of SQL Profiler is to identify slow or resource-intensive queries. To do this, use the default event classes (AuditLogon, AuditLogout, ExistingConnection, RPC:Completed and SQL:BatchCompleted) but add additional columns for DatabaseID and EndTime. For more detailed monitoring (individual statements) add event classes SP:StmtCompleted and SQL:StmtCompleted.

There are many other event classes including transactions, blocking and execution plans but they are outside the scope of this document.

For monitoring blocking, we recommend the stored procedure sp_blocker_pss80 which is downloadable from Microsoft (http://support.microsoft.com/kb/271509)

Overheads

When using SQL Profiler the following issues should be considered:

- There can be significant overheads if the SQL server is busy and SQL Profiler is set to capture a wide range of event classes, and in this case Profiler reports dropped events

- When running SQL Profiler remotely you must bear in mind that all trace data is pulled back across the network

- SQL Profiler running on the SQL Server has a CPU overhead

- 'Server processes SQL server trace data' option in SQL Profiler avoids dropped events but creates higher overhead on SQL server process

- Internal SQL trace causes the lowest overhead

Two tips to consider are:

- To avoid system impact, always write to a trace file on a dedicated or low use disk

- For long-term monitoring have a procedure for compressing and archiving trace files

Correlation

The following correlation can be achieved:

- SQL Profiler to Network Trace – TextData column in the SQL trace can be matched to the TCP contents of the client request in a network trace

- SQL Profiler to Network Trace – The internal SQL process id (SPID) can be matched to a TCP session using the SPID field in the Buffer Header of a TDS packet from the SQL server

- SQL Profiler to client Perfmon – the Client Process ID appears in the Profiler entries and in Process objects in Perfmon running on the client machine

See *Tabular Data Stream Protocol Specification* from Microsoft for more information.

Other Tools

If the problem is within a server or PC here are some other tools you might use:

- Xperf – An extremely powerful tool that collects data from many sources within the Windows operating system

- ApiMon – Calls made across the Win32 API.

- TdiMon – Transport Driver Interface calls (effectively WinSock activity)

- strace – API, process and I/O tracing for UNIX systems

With these tools you can further narrow the fault domain of the problem.

Grades of Diagnostic Data

In the subsections above we have touched on the use of statistics as Definitive Diagnostic Data, and this leads us to the concept of diagnostic data grades which are analogous to types of evidence at criminal law.

Grade A	Time-stamped request/response trace between functional units	Witness
Grade B	Statistics relating to error rates, utilisation, queue lengths, queue service times, response time, etc. where: a) the statistics are synchronised to the symptom events b) fine granularity of sample intervals, such as 1 second	Circumstantial
Grade C	Uncorrelated monitor statistics relating to error rates, utilisation, queue lengths, response time, etc.	Hearsay

Whilst the use of statistical data for troubleshooting may not be as good as time-stamped events, statistics framed within certain rules are very useful. An added advantage is that statistics are more readily available in an enterprise environment and more widely understood by IT operations people.

The grading of data and, in particular, the use of Grade B data is a theme being explored in the development of RPR v2.04.

Definitive Diagnostic Data Collection

Successful collection of DDD is key to the effectiveness of RPR. In this section we'll take a look at three techniques that can be used to develop a reliable and effective DCP.

Binary Chop

This is a simple technique that can literally slice through the problem. The network analyser is an excellent tool to use for this as it can be used to slice the system at a physical component level. Once you have determined the component then you would use further tools to drill-down within it e.g. SQL trace tool if the problem is in the database server.

As an example, consider the following scenario. You are asked to investigate the cause of a network problem (at least that's what you are told the problem is).

Figure 23 Binary chop example

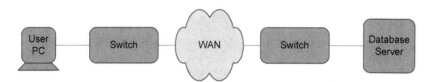

After some initial information gathering you discover the real problem is that a number of users are intermittently losing their network drives. How do you approach the problem?

At a low level there are probably hundreds of possible causes.

Figure 24 Binary chop tree

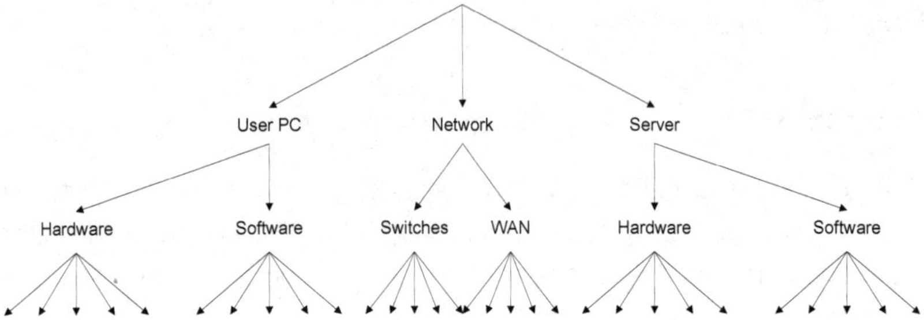

When using the Binary Chop technique your starting point is simply to consider three fundamental functional units; the Client, the Network and the Server. Provided we have a reasonable understanding of the interactions between two functional units we determine if one or the other is the cause of a problem.

In this example, as a first step the correct place to chop through the system is at the PCs interface to the network. By analysing the traffic going to and from the client PC we can determine if the fault is with the PC or with the rest of the system.

If the problem is in the rest of the system we use Binary Chop to determine if it is a network or server problem by analysing at the interface between the two. If it's a server problem we move down that branch and determine if it's hardware or software. And so on.

	Where to make the first chop
	For the first pass, always chop at a boundary where it is simplest to correlate the occurrence of the symptom with trace data events. This is commonly at a boundary close to the user.

Diagnostic capture at the server will result in an awful lot of trace data from all the users of that server. Even if a user notifies the Problem Analyst immediately they have a problem, there will be many diagnostic events following the point of failure. By choosing to study close to the user first, it is possible to see what the user is doing and mark diagnostic data at the moment the problem occurs. Once the data flows associated with the problem are understood at this point in the system it's easier to plan for capture at other points.

The final level at which we need to chop the system will depend upon the support responsibility for the functional units each side of the chop point.

First Principles

Any functional unit will normally remain in its present state unless one of two things happen:

- An internal event causes a change – for example a timer popping, I/O completing or a hardware fault, OR

- An external event causes a change. This can mean anything from someone pressing a button on the front panel, the functional unit receiving a command to an abnormal reaction to normal data

You should never lose sight of these simple facts. Yes, a programming exception could occur, but this is unlikely without some form of other event to make the box run through the faulty code.

Working Alongside the User

When studying a problem that manifests itself as a symptom on a user PC, the Problem Analyst should locate themselves near one or more of the affected users. The advantages are:

- The IT Department is seen to be taking the problem seriously, which usually goes down very well with users and is a good political move

- The Problem Analyst knows immediately when a problem occurs – this helps to avoid the wrapping of diagnostic data and enables the timely creation of markers

- You can ask the user exactly what they did leading up to the problem

The last point is particularly powerful. Take copious notes and include details such as:

- The menu options selected and how (clicked on File, clicked on Open, clicked on drop-down button to give a list of Drives, chose a network drive, etc.)

- Data entered by the user (typed "forecast may 09.doc" into the File Name box, pressed OK)

- The data that was on the screen at the point of failure

	Understanding the scenario
	The more you know about what the user did leading up to the problem, the easier it will be to interpret the diagnostic data.

Date and Time Synchronisation

Time Synchronisation reduces the time needed to analyse and interpret trace data. The techniques set out here help the Problem Analyst synchronise data sources and deal with time sync problems.

Initial Synchronisation

Time is critical to the analysis of diagnostic data:

- Absolute time is used to identify the occurrence of a specific incident and establish the order of diagnostic and other events leading up to the incident

- Relative time is used to determine the delay across functional units and the response time of systems, servers and services

The diagnostic tools used with RPR generate data very quickly – often hundreds of thousands of individual events in a single second. RPR requires data that can be correlated directly with a user's experience of the problem (Definitive Diagnostic Data). Correlating hundreds of thousands of diagnostic events from multiple sources both with each other and with the occurrence of a problem is very challenging. Synchronising the time of day of each diagnostic source is a great help.

Perfect synchronisation is not attainable, particularly if it involves a manual procedure. It's also a fact that the clocks in computer-based equipment drift, often at different rates which means two devices are soon out of sync. Synchronisation within a few seconds is adequate, but the closer the better. We will see later how Markers can be used to correlate diagnostic events from multiple sources more closely.

Synchronising standalone tools such as network analysers, performance probes and fibre channel analysers can be achieved by synchronising each device to:

- a reference server within the symptom environment, OR
- the speaking clock.

Synchronising a device to a reference server can be achieved simply by asking a colleague to countdown to a particular time.

Noting the Time Difference

It's not always possible to synchronise the diagnostic data sources. Typically Windows servers, UNIX server and network equipment in a symptom environment will not be time synchronised. In this case use one server as a reference and note the time difference between the diagnostic data sources and the reference server.

The effect of clock drift over a long period of capture is significant, making subsequent analysis difficult. For this reason, if days, weeks or months pass between the initiation of diagnostic data capture and the eventual occurrence of the problem, careful note should be taken of the time differences between the data sources once the captures are stopped.

If time synchronisation of the equipment at the time of capture is forgotten, don't give up on the idea. Check the time differences as soon as it's realised that this vital information is missing.

	Synchronise date and time
	Within practical limits, synchronise the date and time of the analysers you use. This will speed up trace analysis by narrowing the range of trace entries that you need to study.
	If this is not possible make a careful note of the time differences between diagnostic data sources.

Synchronisation Based On Infrequent Events

It's often possible to synchronise two sets of diagnostic data based on an infrequent or unusual event. Two examples are:

- Synchronise a network trace to a web server log by finding a particular login event, or the execution of an infrequently-used page

- Synchronise a network trace to a SQL server trace by finding a particular login, or the execution of an infrequently-used stored procedure

This approach can be enhanced by scrutinising patterns of events. If, in one data capture you see a login, a 2 second gap, then another login, a further 15 second gap and then a final login, you can look for this same pattern in another data capture. Looking at the timestamps for these events in each data capture enables you to calculate the time difference between the two.

Markers

Marking is possibly the most important of all the RPR techniques. It enables the Problem Analyst to correlate symptoms to data, and to match data from one source to data from another. This section describes some simple but powerful marking techniques.

Introduction

Markers are diagnostic data events generated under the control of the Problem Analyst (or of someone on her behalf) and generating them is an important technique in RPR. Markers fulfil two key roles:

- A marker sent at the time of a problem means that diagnostic data can be matched to a user experience

- Markers sent at any time can be used to synchronise diagnostic data from multiple sources

As it is difficult to get specific marker software installed into an environment, Advance7 Problem Analysts mainly use facilities commonly found in any IT estate. What follows are examples of makers and their uses.

Network Trace to Network Trace Synchronisation

- Send a ping to a server to mark several network traces

User's Perspective to Network Trace Synchronisation

- Send a ping to a server to mark several network traces

Network Trace to Perfmon Synchronisation

- Add the metric ICMP\Received Echo/sec to a server perfmon study so that a ping can be used to correlate network activity with perfmon counters and Event Log entries

- If the server receives periodic pings from a management system a batch file should be created to send, say, 10 pings in quick succession thereby creating a sharp spike in the ICMP\Received Echo/sec metric

- Other events, invalid or not, can be generated that appear as network traffic and perfmon counted events although care must be taken as some support groups do not like the idea of sending invalid commands to their servers in case it causes an unexpected problem

Network Trace to SQL Trace Synchronisation

- Using Access, create and run an SQL Query for a constant such as: SELECT 'database open failed here' FROM activity LIMIT 1, OR

- Use DTCping to create a marker shot through network traces and SQL trace

Network Trace to Procmon Synchronisation

■ Use the Windows command "type" to list a test file from a network drive to create a marker shot through network and procmon traces

■ Open a non-existent file to create a distinguishable marker in a network and procmon trace

Network Trace to Web Log Synchronisation

■ In Internet Explorer GET a non-existent URL to create a marker shot through network traces and web logs

Network Trace to Application Log Synchronisation

■ Enter invalid but recognisable data in an application form field

■ Use the occurrence of several uncommon events that appear in network traces and application logs (such as application login)

Manual Markers as Delimiters

If a problem can be reproduced at will you have the opportunity to mark the start and end of a failing or slow transaction. This is done by sitting alongside a user, sending one ping when they start a transaction (with say a button click) and another when the transaction has completed and the application is usable again.

It's a good idea to observe use of the application for 10 minutes or so to gain a complete understanding of the user actions and at what point the application is again usable (which is not always obvious). It will also help if you explain to the user what you are doing and ask them to refrain from unnecessary mouse clicks or switching windows during the capture period.

Make accurate notes

Make sure that you record the precise details of when markers are sent. You have to be very clear about the fact that the start marker was definitely sent before the transaction started, or sent slightly after. Similarly, was the end marker sent towards the end of the transaction or definitely after it had completed. This is perhaps the most critical aspect of using markers.

Markers: Comparative Analysis

An additional important use of manual markers is to understand the diagnostic events that occur during a good transaction. By marking the start and end of a good transaction you can:

- Identify all the intervening diagnostic events associated with the transaction

- Identify the event that marks the start and end of a transaction

- Determine methods to correlate data from several sources

- Identify where a bad transaction diverges from a good one

This is a particularly useful technique if bad transactions occur infrequently and so you can't realistically mark the start and end of one.

See Comparative Analysis on page 172.

Automatic Markers as Delimiters

The concept of automatic markers is quite simple. The problem analyst puts in place a mechanism that repeatedly checks if a problem has occurred and the status is shown directly in the diagnostic data. Here are some examples:

- A Windows batch command or script file that repeatedly checks for the existence of a file on a server to determine when it is deleted – the batch commands are run from a PC so that the check and the result can be seen in a network trace

- Perfmon is used to collect statistics remotely from a server every second so that the RPC calls and resulting data appear in a network trace

	Continuous marking
	We had to look at a TCP disconnect problem where sessions to certain (random) parts of a network were lost. We set up a batch program to append time and then the results of a ping to a PING.LOG. The batch file was set in a loop to generate a ping every second. The ping target was a router along the path from the client to the server. When the disconnect occurred we could see that the path to the router was not working and could match the trace to the failing ping.

Important Note

When using markers it's important to get firm control of the activity immediately the problem happens. The scenario should be:

- Ask the user to completely stop using their PC at the time of the problem and immediately notify you

- Send the marker

- Note exactly at what point the marker was sent e.g. during the hang, immediately after the error, etc.

- Record as much information as possible from the user's screen

- Ask the user for the precise actions that led to the problem and record them

- Note any data that the user input for the failing or slow transaction

- Now and only now tell the user that they are free to continue working

If the problem can be recreated at will:

- Send a beginning marker

- Ask the user to recreate the problem in a very controlled and neat way (not flicking between applications while waiting, etc.)

- Mark the end of the transaction or the point where an error occurs

It's almost guaranteed that new RPR Practitioners will fail to control and note the conditions under which the markers are sent. It's only after going through hours of frustrating analysis that they will realise the importance of this aspect of markers. The more known about the marker scenario the easier it will be to analyse the diagnostic data.

Managing Diagnostic Data

It's easy to become overwhelmed by the amount of data collected. Whilst the contents of each file may be obvious at the time of capture, details are soon forgotten. The few simple rules listed here help the Problem Analyst manage diagnostic data in a way that aids later analysis.

When formulating the Diagnostic Capture Plan it's important to lay down some rules regarding the management of the collected data.

- **Establish a Naming Convention.** This may include information such as the userid or IP address that the data pertains to. Inclusion of date and time in ISO format (e.g. 2008_04_25 11_22) is also useful. Although the Last Modified time and date can be used, if the file is filtered or modified in any way this information is lost.

- **Use Standard File Extensions.** Use the file extension that is the default for the equipment or diagnostic software being used. When analysing diagnostic files it is extremely annoying to have to choose an application from a list or override the system default repeatedly.

- **Make Copious Notes.** At the time of collection be sure to make a note of what each set of diagnostic data files contains. At the time of capture it's easy to remember what's what, but the following day it may be very difficult.

- **Always Keep an Original Copy.** When analysing diagnostic data always keep an original copy of the data on a memory stick or CD. This is valuable data and may be very hard to re-create. Protect it like any other important data.

- **Manage Free Disk and Memory Space.** It is very easy to fill a disk with diagnostic data. If a problem is intermittent, capture of the data may be on an unattended device. When you first start the capture, assess the rate at which the disk is filling and hence the maximum time that can be spanned. If possible, use a ring buffer configuration so that older data is overwritten but be sure that the eventual captured amount will span the time needed.

Event Capture Procedure Issues

A few simple tips can improve the effectiveness of an ECP. Here are a couple of tips to help busy Problem Analysts collect essential information at the time of a problem.

Note Taking

Take copious notes no matter how scruffy. Details of timings, names, precise wording of messages, etc. are a big advantage when performing a web search or writing up a Status Report. If a supplier can see the details of an error message in the Status Report verbatim they will know that this is not just anecdotal evidence.

 Collecting configuration details

This is a simple but very powerful tip for the collection of configuration details. Most active network components have a management port or allow TELNET access for command line management. Use a terminal emulator with logging capabilities (even Windows Terminal can do this). Start logging, run through a full sequence of commands to display the configuration information and then stop logging. You know have all the details and can cut and paste the appropriate parts into your Status Report. Redirecting command output is also a very useful way to collect configuration and release. For example:

```
c:\>  ipconfig /all >> c:\temp\ipconfig.txt
c:\>  route print >> c:\temp\route.txt
c:\>  nbstat -n >> c:\temp\nbstat-n.txt
c:\>  driverquery >> c:\temp\driverquery.txt
```

You may also want to consider copying important config files, for example:

- Windows – Event Log, \windows\system32\drivers\etc\hosts, etc.

- UNIX – /etc/networks, /etc/hosts, /etc/named.boot, the other DNS files, etc.

Collecting such data will save you a lot of time when dealing with suppliers. Create a specific directory so that all the information can be deposited in one place. Having a baseline copy of these files can also be helpful if you suspect unexpected changes are occurring.

Data Collection by Others

If a problem is very intermittent it is unlikely that a member of the PSG will be on-hand 24 x 7 to handle the diagnostic data collection. Therefore, it may be necessary to rely on others to stop and save data collection, or record some other information.

It's important to insist on tight control of any actions to be carried out by others. A typical scenario might be one where you ask a Service Desk technician to take a verbatim note of the error before he attempts to recover the situation and to save the PC Event Log. A day later, the Service Desk call to say that the problem has occurred, the required information has been collected and the information has been emailed to the appropriate PSG member. Upon reviewing the data it's obvious that the error message hasn't been recorded isn't listed anywhere and the Event Log shows a whole sequence of events that weren't expected. A call to the Service Desk technician reveals,

---

"I didn't do exactly what you said. I was in a hurry so I got the user working again and dumped the Event Log soon after that. I didn't write down the message but I'm sure that it said something about a network failure – you know the one."

The information is probably useless and you'll have to wait for the next failure.

If data collection can go wrong it will. Make sure that you provide a written step-by-step Event Capture Procedure to everyone who might have to collect the data. Make the procedure very tight. Allow no room for error. Emphasise to all concerned that unless the procedure is followed EXACTLY the data collected will be useless, and this will cause delays in fixing the problem.

Diagnostic Data Analysis

With thousands of captured events from multiple data sources, data analysis can become very challenging. In this section we describe techniques to help the Problem Analyst get a handle on all that data.

Data Map

A Diagnostic Capture Plan can generate an awful lot of data. If the plan generates multiple capture files from many capture points, or if the files contain multiple examples of the problem it is a good idea to create a map. The simplest way of doing this is to create a spreadsheet with a row for each example of the problem. The columns should be:

- Description of the problem

- Time of the problem

- User name, userid and/or IP address

- Capture Point 1 files

- Capture Point 1 event record numbers

- Capture Point 1 time offset

- Capture Point 2 files

- Capture Point 2 event record numbers

- Capture Point 2 time offset

- etc.

Although the description of the problem should be the same in each case (i.e. the Chosen Symptom), the description may include brief details of the scenario such as "Customer Search by ID took 25 seconds – Customer ID was 1234567". The capture file and record number information provides the start and end points of the problem transaction within the diagnostic data.

Figure 25 Diagnostic data map

Time of Problem	Description	IP Address	PC		Check Point eth2	
			File & Record Range	Time Offset	File & Record Range	Time Offset
16:01	IE freeze for 24s after clicking on Show Flights	xx.171.90.185	pc_20091017155523 4256 to 5358	00:00:00.000	fw_20091017155416 1733 to 1916	0C:00:00.000

This idea can be expanded further to match the diagnostic events in each trace In the following example we've used a simple spreadsheet to summarise network trace entries from two sources in an eCommerce environment.

Figure 26   eCommerce example

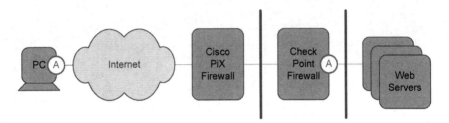

(A) Network Trace Capture Points

Above is a simplified diagram of an eCommerce website used to book airline flights. Whilst booking a flight the user pauses mid-booking to find his credit card. The user returns to his PC to continue with the booking but Internet Explorer hangs for about 24 seconds after clicking the button to book a selected flight.

The problem was re-creatable, and so network traces were captured at the time of a problem by running Wireshark on the PC and using tcpdump on one of the firewalls. Although the network trace captured at the PC had a hundred or so entries, the trace taken from the firewall contained approximately 200,000 frames. Filtering techniques were used to reduce both traces to around 50 packets. On the face of it, analysis of traces of this size should be simple, but:

■ One trace was not a frame-by-frame match for the other

■ The timestamps were different

■ The client PC IP address and TCP port number were transposed

This made it difficult to get an overall view of the data flows in the system. To provide a high level view summary information from each trace was used to create a spreadsheet.

Figure 27   Diagnostic event summary

			PC			Check Point eth2		
Ref	Dir	Detail	Frame	Time	Client Port	Frame	Time	Client Port
1	-->	Get /book/index.asp	4256	16:00:53.424	53287	1733	16:00:11.596	13349
2	<--	200 OK - First of a 20 pkt seq	4258	16:00:53.424	53287	1735	16:00:11.744	13349
3	<--	Last of the 20 pkt sequence	4285	16:00:53.608	53287	1762	16:00:11.775	13349
4	-->	[ACK]	4286	16:00:53.608	53287	1763	16:00:11.779	13349
5	<--	[RST] - origin = web server				1909	16:02:23.176	13349
6	-->	POST /book/step1.asp – pt1	5170	16:03:01.764	53287			
7	-->	POST /book/step1.asp – pt2	5171	16:03:01.764	53287			
8	-->	POST /book/step1.asp – pt1	5181	16:03:02.006	53287			
9	-->	POST /book/step1.asp – pt1	5189	16:03:02.655	53287			
10	-->	POST /book/step1.asp – pt1	5198	16:03:03.856	53287			
11	-->	POST /book/step1.asp – pt1	5213	16:03:06.256	53287			
12	-->	POST /book/step1.asp – pt1	5226	16:03:08.656	53287			
13	-->	POST /book/step1.asp – pt1	5235	16:03:11.057	53287			
14	-->	POST /book/step1.asp – pt1	5253	16:03:15.857	53287			
15	-->	[RST] - origin = PC	5350	16:03:25.449	53287			
16	-->	[SYN]	5351	16:03:25.452	53300	1910	16:02:43.624	14185
17	<--	[SYN,ACK]	5353	16:03:25.457	53300	1911	16:02:43.624	14185
18	-->	[ACK]	5354	16:03:25.457	53300	1912	16:02:43.628	14185
19	-->	POST /book/step1.asp – pt1	5355	16:03:25.457	53300	1913	16:02:43.629	14185
20	-->	POST /book/step1.asp – pt2	5356	16:03:25.457	53300	1914	16:02:43.629	14185
21	<--	[ACK]	5357	16:03:25.462	53300	1915	16:02:43.630	14185
22	<--	302 Object Moved	5358	16:03:25.476	53300	1916	16:02:43.644	14185

This made it much simpler to visualize the problem and explain it to others. Here's the sequence of events using the Ref number to keep track:

- 1 to 4 – Normal activity on a single TCP session (note the change of Client Port numbers)

- 5 – After an idle period of more than 2 minutes the web server RESETs the TCP connection, however the RESET packet is not seen at the PC

- 6 and 7 – the user clicks the button and Internet Explorer tries to send data to the web server on the TCP session it was using earlier

- 8 to 14 – Internet Explorer repeatedly tries to send the data on the original TCP connection

- 15 – Internet Explorer assumes there is a problem and RESETs the connection

- 16 to 18 – Internet Explorer starts a new connection

- 19 and 20 – Internet Explorer sends the data via the new TCP connection

- 21 – the web server acknowledges receipt of the data

- 22 – the web server sends the correct reply

It is quite obvious from the spreadsheet that the root cause of this problem is the fact that the RESET at Ref 5 did not get sent to the PC, and so the PC believed that the original TCP connection was still available for use. Gaining this level of understanding without summarizing the traces in this way would have been difficult.

The time offset is critical to matching diagnostic data from multiple sources. Designate one source as the reference and note the time difference from this reference. In the example above the PC time was used as the reference and we can see that the timestamp on the PC trace is approximately 42 seconds ahead of that of the firewall trace.

Timeline

Once the start and end points of the problem transaction have been established it's a good idea to list the major events within those boundaries and the times that those events occurred. Without a timeline of events is quite easy to arrive at the wrong conclusion.

To illustrate this idea let's consider a slow website transaction. In this example we have web server logs from the time of the problem together with database trace data.

Figure 28   Timeline example

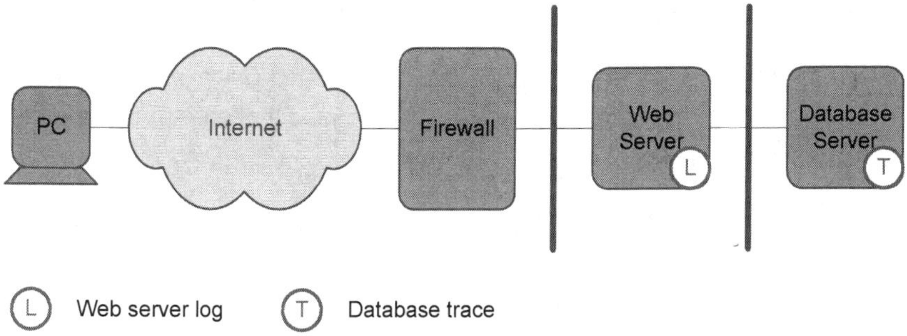

(L) Web server log   (T) Database trace

We've found the HTTP GET command for the slow web page in the web server log, and combining this with the database trace data we find the following:

■ The web page response time was 15 seconds

■ We see various database calls that complete in under 0.2 seconds

■ There is one database Stored Procedure call around the same time that took 13.7 seconds to complete

The 13.7-second Stored Procedure looks like the main culprit until we actually map the events out in a timeline and find the following:

- 11:20:06 – GET command for the slow page is received by the web server

- 11:20:07 – The web server makes four calls to the database and all complete within 0.2 seconds

- 11:20:21 – The web server sends the user the page for the GET command

- 11:20:22 – The web server makes a Stored Procedure call to the database which takes 13.7 seconds to complete

Unless we have made a mistake, the 13.7-second SP execution can't be associated with our slow GET command because it occurred after we sent the web page back to the user.

Milestones

By identifying a few key events in a system and capturing good and bad scenarios, a Problem Analyst can quickly home in on a performance problem.

The concept of establishing an accurate timeline of events can be extended to provide a high level view of a performance problem. To illustrate we'll look at an extreme case where the issue relates to the starting of a PC. Normally, from power up through login to being presented the desktop takes about 90 seconds. Intermittently it takes more than 200 seconds.

A network analyser was used to capture the PCs interactions with servers and services during a normal startup and a slow example. By picking common events in the two traces it was possible to identify common milestones.

Figure 29 Milestones

Mile-	Elapsed Time including Login			Elapsed Time without Login			
stone	Normal	Slow	Diff.	Normal	Slow	Diff.	Description
0	0.000	0.000	0.000	0.000	0.000	0.000	First SMB access to an external
1	11.474	32.860	21.386	11.474	32.860	21.386	Last SMB open prior to presentation of login dialogue box
2	122.533	48.091	-74.442	11.474	32.860	21.386	First SMB command after completion of the login dialogue
3	123.969	49.813	-74.156	12.910	34.582	21.672	Completion of access to gpt.ini
4	126.383	131.551	5.168	15.324	116.320	100.996	First access to \srvsvc
5	129.235	135.616	6.381	18.176	120.385	102.209	Execution of pgpstatus.vbs
6	137.477	146.269	8.792	26.418	131.038	104.620	First access to \inventory\DESKTOP14367-20084463837.txt
7	143.791	190.918	47.127	32.732	175.687	142.955	First access to \w32\whatsup\message.rtf
8	180.313	225.555	45.242	69.254	210.324	141.070	First access to \107533\.....\Outlook\outcmd.dat

Above we see some of those milestones together with the elapsed time for Normal and Slow starts. The user took differing amounts of time to login in each case. To eliminate this variation we adjusted the figures for zero time to login (the without Login set of figures). Plotting the resulting figures immediately shows the area of the problem.

Figure 30 Time delay between milestones

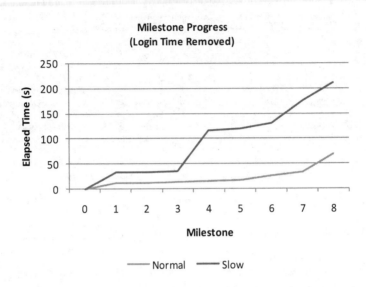

Milestone Progress
(Login Time Removed)

There is an additional 79 second delay between milestones 3 and 4 in the slow startup example, and so this is obviously the area in which we need to focus.

Similar timelines to this can be established for any diagnostic data to help narrow the data range.

Comparative Analysis

This technique is probably as old as problem diagnosis itself. Following a few simple rules the Problem Analyst can successfully incorporate this technique into a DCP and subsequent Diagnostic Analysis Plan.

The 'slow PC startup' example above demonstrates the use of Comparative Analysis. To determine the area of the problem we compare the diagnostic events for a problem scenario with those for a normal scenario. This is a useful technique to use when the abnormal traffic patterns that are causing or are resulting from the problem are not obvious.

Comparative Analysis can be slow for a couple of reasons:

- There can be minor variations between the good and bad scenarios that mean that the diagnostic captures don't match for this reason alone

- When good and bad diagnostic captures differ it can take some time to determine if this is significant

The following points are a good guide to the side-by-side analysis of good and bad diagnostic captures:

- The good and bad diagnostic captures should be compared in strict time order

- As each difference is identified it must be investigated and explained

- Work through the data in chronological order to find the first point where the bad scenario differs from the good one, but there is no reasonable explanation for the difference – consider this as the first indication of a problem and investigate

- Although subsequent diagnostic events may be of general interest, don't get too hung up on these – any activity following an error is likely to be very different from normal simply because an error has occurred

Analysing Performance Problems

IT performance can appear complicated which can make the development of a DCP more difficult than it need be. In this section we present the Problem Analyst with the fundamentals of IT performance from an RPR perspective.

Performance Basics

Background

The performance of an end-to-end system is dependent on five factors; technology, design, load, recoverable errors and dynamic reconfiguration.

Figure 31 Response time elements

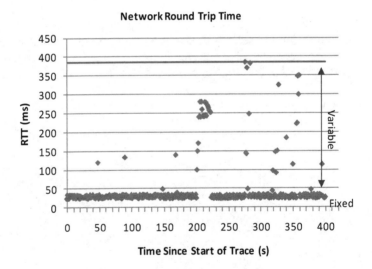

The fixed portion of response time (and the minimum value) is determined by:

■ Technology – Speed of light, server processor speed, bits per second transferred, time across a switch backplane, time taken to execute code, etc.

■ Design – Application, clustering, location of servers, etc. – Things that might overcome technology limitations or make them worse!

The variable portion of response time is determined by:

■ Queuing – Due to network load, CPU utilisation, disk I/O rate, prioritisation policies, etc.

■ Recoverable Errors – Dropped packets, database lock contention, name resolution time-outs, etc.

■ Dynamic Configuration Change – Intended or incorrect dynamic changes to the configuration of a system such as change of storage path, switch into backup network path, etc.

Technology

Whether it is the time taken to execute CPU instructions, or the time taken to clock data onto and off a network channel, all technologies introduce delays. Some are immutable, such as the speed of light. Although individually the delays may be small, they become significant if they occur many times. Disk access time may be around 4ms, and so if an application transaction requires 5,000 physical disk reads total response time could be greater than 20s.

International networking often offers the greatest challenge. A typical round-trip network delay from Singapore to London is 200ms. An additional 200ms on top of a transaction response time of say 2 seconds is unlikely to bother any user. However, if completion of the transaction requires 100 trips backwards and forwards (often called network turns) the 2-second transaction suddenly weighs in at 22 seconds.

An upgrade may solve a problem by reducing processing time, disk queuing or serialisation delay. Other limitations are just a fact of life – the speed of light being the prime example.

Design

Design can overcome the technology limitations. Disk caching might significantly reduce the effects of disk access time. Network protocols can sometimes eliminate the multiplier effect of network turns. Application and solution design can also overcome network turn effects. For example, applications that use a web browser for the user interface are usually less susceptible the multiplier effects of network turns.

Queuing and Recoverable Errors

If the application performance is consistent but slow, no matter what time of the day or night you try it, the issue is probably related to the technology in use and the design.

If performance is occasionally or mostly unacceptable an overload condition that is causing queuing or a high rate of recoverable errors are the most likely causes.

It can be tricky to separate load and recoverable errors as overload conditions can lead to recoverable errors. For example, if the rate of disk I/O request overloads a Fibre Channel switch port, frames are queued within the switch until they can be sent. If the queue reaches a preset maximum size any further frames are simply dropped. This causes a recoverable error condition.

Dynamic Configuration Changes

Dynamic changes occur in systems to:

- Bypass failing components – such as failover from a primary database server to a standby server

- Balance load across resources – such as moving a virtual machine to another host

- Increase resources – such increasing the pool of TCP connections to a database

Many of these changes are automated and so log information that records such changes is an important clement of the diagnostic data available.

Beware of Wiggly Graphs

Gathering utilisation figures for servers and network components is a great way to identify obvious overload problems. An obvious network overload will show as a utilisation graph that is solidly stuck above 70%. This doesn't guarantee that the network load is the cause of your performance problem but it does indicate that more capacity is needed.

Figure 32 Wiggly graph

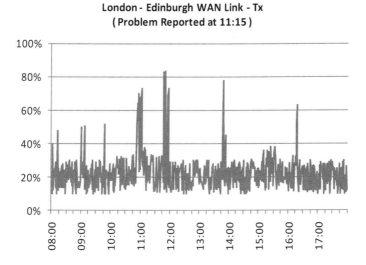

However be sceptical of anyone who diagnoses the cause of a performance problem solely from a wiggly graph – the sort that swings up and down or has lots of spikes. Server and network load is very bursty, and spiky graphs are common (even right up to 100%). Although such graphs are very useful to manage server and network capacity, be very careful using them to fix problems – particularly intermittent problems. If an overload condition is not obvious use other techniques such as time accounting to confirm the cause of the performance problem.

Conclusions

Technology limitations will determine the best level of performance that can be achieved. Load, recoverable errors and dynamic reconfiguration will cause variations in performance. Design will affect the best level of performance and the degree of variation.

Most performance problems can be solved by a methodical check for evidence of the five causes of technology, design, queuing, recoverable errors and dynamic reconfiguration. Certain types of problem can be difficult to diagnose, such as:

- Transient overload conditions

- Intermittent recoverable errors

- Technology limitations

- Design issues

RPR is very effective in these cases.

Response Times

Response time is obviously one of the key metrics affecting the end-user's satisfaction with an application. In this section we extend the use of the response time metric to analyse the performance of the components that make up an application.

Request-Response Pairs

The majority of network protocols send messages in pairs:

- a client entity sends a request to a server or service

- the service processes the request and then sends a response back to the client

Based on this simple principle, the performance of the server or service can then be expressed as a response time; that being the difference between the time the request is sent to the service and the time the response is received.

Response Times and Fault Domains

By measuring the response time at the network interface between functional units we can quickly gain an understanding of the cause of a performance problem.

Figure 33 Functional Unit 2 issue

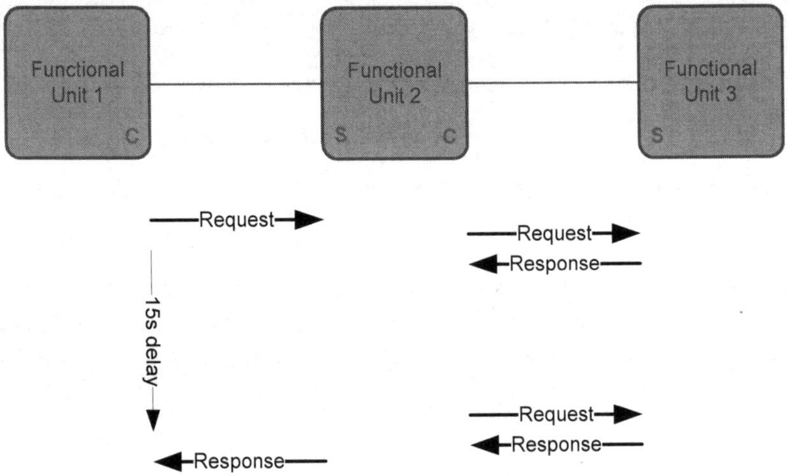

In the above diagram consider that time is increasing down the page. We can see that there is a 15 second response time experienced by FU1 (Functional Unit 1). To fulfil the request from FU1, FU2 must request data from FU3. It's evident that there is a delay between the request-response pairs from FU2 to FU3, and therefore the majority of the response time is down to a delay in FU2.

Note here, that if you conclude that the delay is within FU2 you are assuming that FU2 doesn't interact with something else that may, in fact, be causing the delay. Care needs to be taken when devising a DCP and analysing the collected data to ensure we identify all interactions.

Figure 34   Functional Unit 3 issue

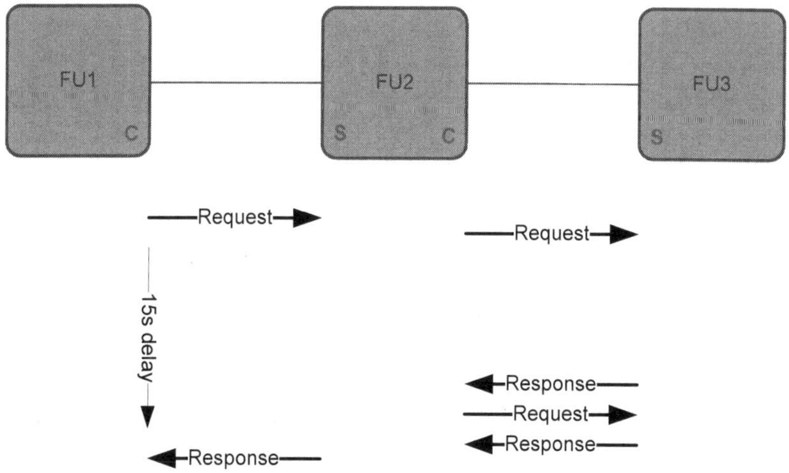

In this example we see that there is a delay between a request from Functional Unit 2 and the response from Functional Unit 3. In this case the majority of the response time is down to a delay in Functional Unit 3.

Figure 35   Network issue

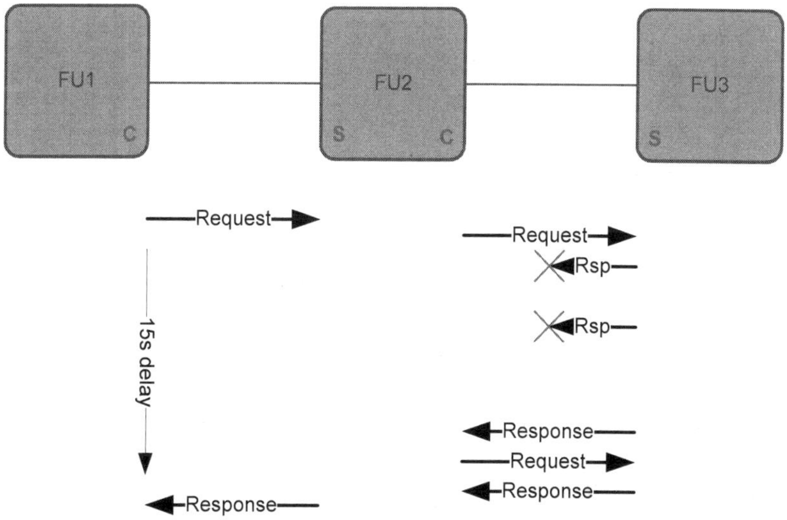

In the example we see that although Functional Unit 3 responds quickly to all requests from Functional Unit 2, the first response is lost by the network. Functional Unit 3 resends the response but this message is also lost by the network. Functional Unit 3 tries to send the response a third time and on this occasion it is successfully received by Functional Unit 2 and the data flows continue as normal.

TCP/IP Practicalities

In a system using TCP/IP for communication between the functional units control messages (i.e. messages not carrying application data) are used to acknowledge data messages. When a client or server sends a message it expects to receive an acknowledgement (ACK) within a certain period of time, known as a timeout. If the ACK doesn't arrive the sender assumes the original message was lost and so sends it again. When using TCP/IP the timeouts can add up to large delays as the timeout value doubles with each retry. For a more detailed explanation of the acknowledgement mechanism see *TCP/IP Essentials* on page 211.

When studying a TCP/IP trace showing these types of interactions there are two points to consider.

Applications that use TCP/IP create connections between client and server. These connections are often called sessions. The TCP/IP flows between two functional units (say between an application server and a database) may be carried on many TCP sessions. The principles described in this section must be applied on a session-by-session basis. Network analysers provide filter capabilities to display only those packets associated with one session. In Wireshark this is achieved by right clicking on a packet in the Summary window that is flowing on the session we are interested in and then choosing Follow TCP Stream.

We also need to remove any control messages that are not carrying application data. We can do this by simply filtering the trace to remove all packets that have a zero TCP payload length. In Wireshark the filter is tcp.len>0.

Time Accounting

When faced with an intermittent performance problem, technical support people are likely to suggest many theoretical causes. Thankfully the Problem Analyst can avoid pursuing theories and provide hard evidence of the causes of a slow response time using this technique.

The Principle

Time accounting is an analysis technique to locate the cause of a performance problem by identifying the time spent in each functional unit of an end-to-end system. Time accounting is based on the fundamental fact that the response time experienced by an application user is made up of the delay introduced by each component of the end-to-end system. Therefore, one way of determining the cause of an excessive response time is to measure the time introduced by every component, find those components contributing the most and drill down into them further.

Figure 36   Time account

	Time Contribution (s)	
User PC		-0.049
WAN		1.522
Web Server		
- Central DB	10.779	
- Branch DB	2.476	
- Other	0.000	
- Application	0.299	
		13.554
		15.027

The above example (used again later in this book) is a good example of the technique. We can see that of a total response time of 15.027 seconds, 10.779 seconds is spent in the Central Database. This gives us an instant indication of where to investigate further.

Response Times

When considering the performance aspects of a business application, the most important response time is that experienced by the user. It is usually considered to be the time taken from when the user submitted a request to an application by hitting the Return key or clicking on a button to the point where the application is ready to accept another request. The user response time is made up of:

- Client PC Time – the time the client application needs to process the request and deal with the response

- Server Time – the time spent in one or more servers required by the application

- Service Time – the time spent in an external service

- Network Time – the time spent transferring data between;
  - Client PC and server
  - Client PC and service
  - Two servers
  - A server and a service

In many cases the user response time is the sum of all the times listed above.

Figure 37 Response time components

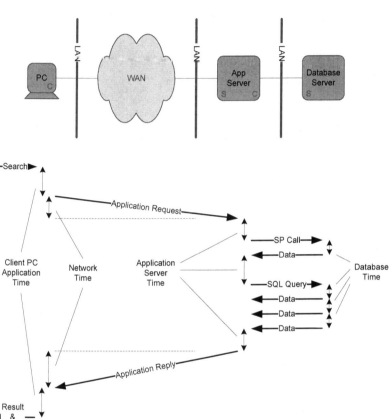

In the example above the user clicks on the Search button of an application and after a delay (User Transaction Response Time) gets sees the Result of the search and the window is Unlocked ready for a new transaction. We can see that the User Transaction Response Time on the far left is made up as follows:

```
User Transaction RT = Client PC Application Time
                    + Network Time
                    + Application Server Time
                    + Database Time
```

Also note that each tier of the end–to-end system can be thought of as a Client-Server configuration (note the red C and S characters). You could even consider the user as a Client of the service provided by the Client PC.

The simple addition of the response times for each sub-transaction from the Client PC time may not yield the correct result. Factors that affect the calculation are:

- The overlapping of multiple sub-transactions which means that some work is performed in parallel

- Caching techniques that mean that some sub-transactions are not necessary

In the latter case, caching would be accounted for within the total time spent in the application server.

Application, Server and Service Response Times

At a fundamental level the response time of an application, server or service can be determined by looking at the interactions of the transport-level protocol, for example TCP. Therefore in the example above you can use network analysers to determine how much time is contributed by each component of a system. The contribution is;

a) the sum of the time differences between requests to the component and the corresponding responses, less

b) the sum of the time differences between requests the component sends to other components and the matching responses.

Figure 38   Response time contribution

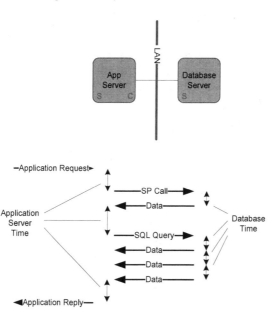

To illustrate the technique consider the above example. To complete a transaction the application server retrieves data from a database server. The response time contribution from the database is determined by simply looking at the time difference between the Stored Procedure (SP) Call or SQL Query arriving at the server and the data being returned.

The difference between the time that the Application Request arrives at the application server and the time the Application Reply leaves the server gives a total response time contribution of the application server, LAN and database server. The LAN time is typically insignificant and can be ignored at this stage. The time spent in the application server can be calculated as follows:

```
Application Server Time = Application Response Time
                        - Application Request Time
                        - Database Server Time
```

Multi-Trace Correlation and Time Accounting

Extending the dual trace concept, it's possible to capture definitive diagnostics at multiple points in an end-to-end system. This is a particularly useful approach when investigating a slow response time problem.

Figure 39   Multi-point diagnostic capture

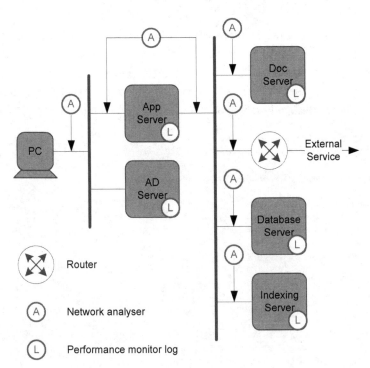

Router

Network analyser

Performance monitor log

In the above example we see that network analysers are placed along the data flow paths to capture interactions between devices. A point of note is the use of a dual port analyser (analyser with dual NIC), to capture requests and responses to and from the User PC and requests from the Application Server to the other servers. By using a dual port analyser the traffic on each side of the Application Server is time synchronised.

	Multi-NIC network analysers
	If you need to capture traffic at multiple points in a network, where possible use an analyser with multiple NICs. The data rate vs. the capture rate must be assessed (check for dropped packets), but if the throughput is sufficient this is a great way to capture time-synchronised diagnostic data.

Soft Skills

Introduction

In this part of the book we look at people skills that are useful when pursuing a problem with RPR. The surprise (or perhaps it's not a surprise) is that the people issues are often far more challenging than the technical issues. There are three particular areas of note:

- IT technical staff are often highly skilled people and suggesting that there may be a better way of tackling a problem is not always easily accepted

- The IT industry has been troubleshooting problems in broadly the same manner for the last 50 years and so RPR represents a significant change

- Solving problems will involve interaction with people (other staff or suppliers) who don't use RPR

In this section we outline techniques that can be used to address the people issues that may be barriers to resolving problems.

Motivation

It's useful to consider the motivating factors for the various people involved in the investigation, diagnosis and resolution of a problem. Different people have differing levels of motivation to get the problem fixed. In general, those most motivated are:

- End-user – The problem is stopping them doing their job,

- Service Delivery Managers – The problem causes repeated tough questions from the business

- Problem Analyst – A challenging puzzle which he or she is paid to solve

- 3rd Line Support – If they enjoy the challenge and have appropriate KPIs relating to end-to-end problem diagnosis

Those less so may be:

- 3rd Line Support – If they don't like working outside their comfort zone or if they'd rather be doing project work

- Supplier – It's a drain on their resources and they'd rather use technical resource to install new solutions

When the issue being tackled is a grey problem there are further issues with the Technical Support Teams in that there is no proof that their technology is to blame and as they are usually overloaded with work, a 3rd Line team may be reluctant to take ownership of a grey problem.

At the time of writing, the author has not yet come across any person in a platform support team who has a KPI relating to end-to-end problem diagnosis.

You also need to consider the fact that some individual or group involved may not want the problem resolved. This may be so because:

- A business case for an upgrade project partly hinges on the fact that it will resolve the problem

- A technical team want to switch to new technology for reasons of kudos or to improve CVs are citing the current problem as the reason for the switch

- One or more contractors rely on repeated incidents for their tenure

- A member of staff or a supplier has built his or her reputation as the person who gets things fixed

These reasons may seem bizarre but they are all real examples of issues that Advance7 has faced when helping clients with problems.

Using the Same Language

As usage shifts from one set of acronyms to another, you should bear In mind that many have been used before. CMS can mean Content Management System or Configuration Management System.

The meaning of certain terms also differs. When someone says that they have an Exchange performance problem is that a Microsoft Exchange problem or a problem with the London Stock Exchange.

Make sure you understand the background of those around you and their terminology. Try to relate things to them in their terms, saving them having to go through the additional brain-loop of decoding what you are saying.

When dealing with a mixed group, stick to one standard such as international standard and framework definitions like ITIL, CCITT or ISO.

A telling meeting
A Problem Analyst went to a meeting at a retail bank to discuss a performance problem. It was 20 minutes into the meeting before he realised that the ATM network they were referring to was their cash-point network and not a cell-based Wide Area Network.

Problems with Pride

If you have been asked to look at a problem that someone else has failed to fix, get that person involved right from the start. There is nothing more soul-destroying than having to admit defeat, particularly having put a tremendous amount of effort into looking at the problem. You can get up to speed quickly using the knowledge of such people, and their local knowledge means that you will rarely be able to fix the problem without them. If you can build a good rapport with them you can speed up the resolution of the problem and restore their confidence. Make sure that all the members of the PSG are seen as part of the solution.

Be careful not to follow your predecessor's train of thought.

A second scenario can occur if you have been brought in as an independent specialist, particularly if you have been commissioned because the engineers from a supplier have been unable to resolve a tricky problem. Pride is seriously injured when someone else enters the equation who is billed as *The Specialist*. Ironically, the same supplier may happily accept the situation if the problem is resolved by one of their regular contacts in the IT department. Tread very lightly and, if possible, include the supplier in the problem resolution.

	Give everyone credit
	Make sure that everyone in the PSG feels as if they had an important role in determining root cause (you can be sure they did), and are seen by the business and project sponsor as being a major contributor.

Ultimately, the Problem Analyst will need the knowledge and skills of others to identify the root cause, and someone else is very likely to be the person to determine the fix. Make sure everyone involved understands these facts.

Overplaying the specialist tag

One of our Problem Analysts made a bit of a mistake while dealing with a problem for a telecommunications company. He was asked to attend a kick-off meeting and explain his approach. He went a little over the top on 'The Specialist' bit – telling everyone at the meeting that he would not be adopting the same approach that they had been, but that he would be using a method called RPR. Without realising it he'd upset three key people in the meeting. He then had to fight them every inch of the way. The problem was resolved, but it took about three weeks when really it should have only taken three or four days.

Selling the Method

The PSG Workshop presents an ideal opportunity to point everyone in the same direction. You must make the problem the common enemy. Describe the problem clearly, being careful not to imply that anyone is to blame. After you have completed the description of the problem on the whiteboard sit down together with everyone else, facing towards the problem.

"Do we all agree that this is the problem?"

Later, when you are deep in the problem, it's always useful to come back to face the whiteboard by way of a progress meeting. Repeatedly identifying the problem will help keep everyone together.

Once you have decided on a Diagnostic Capture Plan you will need to sell it to all. This can be tricky as each member of the PSG may have their own agenda. The best way to sell your approach is to have everyone involved in the formulation of your Diagnostic Capture Plan. Through the PSG Workshop and the Share, Gather, Explain and Sort activity you should be able to reason with all members of the PSG and reach an agreed Diagnostic Capture Plan.

If a supplier, say, has a different Action Plan and you suspect they only have their own objectives in mind, you may have to challenge them by asking how it will determine root cause or resolve the problem. If the supplier produces valid reasons for changing the approach go with their proposal.

There is one other reason that would override your preferred Diagnostic Capture Plan. If you strongly suspect a supplier's piece of kit is the cause and that supplier says he needs a particular trace or set of diagrams you must get them. Make sure that you confirm exactly what's needed in writing.

	A common issue
	There are many books and articles on Problem Solving and they nearly all cite a common cause of failure of a method as the inability to sell it to those involved.

Handling Interruptions

There are two basic types of interruption:

- "Have you made any progress yet?"

- "We've just had this happen"

If Joe is breathing down your neck and repeatedly asking for a status report, set a time for an update. Simply ask if it's OK to meet at 4.30 to discuss progress. He may come back and say, I'll need an update by 3.30, but that's fine – at least you won't be interrupted until that time. But beware:

Don't miss the appointment.

If you do you will destroy all credibility. It's easy to miss it – especially when you are deeply engrossed in a problem but if you feel you will have more to tell Joe if you have an extra thirty minutes to study data, give him a call. He may say he still needs to see you, but at least you have forewarned him that you don't have the answer yet, and he has had the option of waiting a little longer.

The other type of interruption is where Service Desk or support staff hit the Problem Analyst with more and more problems (or symptoms). In this case write a list of the symptoms and ask the person if the priority of each symptom has changed from that set in the last PSG Workshop. Each time a person comes to you with another problem, simply add it to the list. The Problem Analyst does need to take an interruption at this level in case new information has been discovered that is key to solving your problem, but simply adding the problem to a list should avoid getting side tracked by other issues.

If the problem requires all of your attention consider moving from your usual desk into, say, a meeting room. Ask your manager to e-mail users and colleagues explaining that you have been dedicated to fixing the XYZ problem for the next two days and that Jim will be deputising for you. Again there is a PR spin-off here as it's evident that the problem is being taken very seriously.

One problem after another

When Advance7 takes on a new member of staff, we have a development plan that involves training, shadowing, mentoring and gradual introduction to troubleshooting. Unfortunately we are sometimes so busy that the new guy has to wade in sooner than is ideal.

It was on just such an occasion that a new Advance7 Problem Analyst found himself at the offices of a regional newspaper group to investigate a performance problem with the paper's advertising system.

No sooner had the Problem Analyst started looking at the problem than the network manager started bombarding him with more and more problems. The problems were often trivial and he would come back later to say that the problem had been resolved. The Problem Analyst called his manager in frustration:

"I'm getting nowhere. As soon as I start work on one problem he comes to ask me to take a look at another."

On advice, the Problem Analyst met with the network manager and the two wrote out a list of all the problems. Together they prioritised them and the Problem Analyst started his investigations at the top of the list. That was it. The network manager had decided which problem was most urgent, and he knew that the Problem Analyst had a list of the others. The Problem Analyst got some peace and quickly made progress.

Incidents vs. Problems

Repeated incidents can quickly become distracting. Instead of devising and executing a Diagnostic Capture Plan, all the time is consumed reviewing the latest incident. Those around you will often believe that if you look at the latest incident you'll probably come up with the answer. It's a good idea to make sure that everyone understands that your role is to determine the root cause of the problem and not to assist with incident recovery.

Staying Focused

When the pressure is on and you are being bombarded with information, it is very easy to lose focus. Things you are told will interest you and may be relevant to the problem you are looking at, but they could distract you from the agreed plan.

Earlier we considered a scenario of a PC losing its connection to a server.

Figure 40 Staying focused

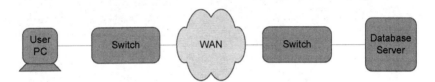

If you recall we decided to use Binary Chop to prove or disprove that the User's PC was failing. Let's say that the first trace you get is inconclusive but you notice something interesting about the operation of the network. That leads you to explore another avenue. You collect more traces relating to this train of thought. At the end of the day you know a lot about the network but you haven't proved or disproved the problem with the PC.

If you go to the next progress meeting and describe how you have discovered some really interesting facts about the way the network handles multicast packets, but you haven't got around to collecting the diagnostic data agreed in the Action Plan, you're unlikely to make friends.

It's worse if you actually leave the site with loads of diagnostic data only to have to return the next day to collect what you need.

Beware the quick win

Even though you may know the advantages of RPR, there is an initial natural urge to look for a quick win – by using the Supporting Techniques, skipping the process and going with gut feel. You may get lucky and resolve the problem in this way, but it's more likely that you won't. Unfortunately this then reinforces the beliefs of those who may have been sceptical of the RPR approach.

Going for the quick win is particularly difficult to resist if those around you are doing just that. The sad irony is that sometimes they will get lucky and fix the problem before you are out of the blocks. However, they probably will never really know the root cause of the problem and at least nine times out of ten RPR will get you to the answer more quickly, particularly as your RPR skills develop.

Handling Pressure

You may also find that the people around you don't understand why you are just sitting there looking at a screen and writing notes. You are unlikely to fix the problem by switching to 'headless chicken' mode, so if a slow considered approach is needed – just do it. If the stern looks get too much you might want to move to another area.

To get some time to think consider going for a walk or slowly getting a coffee. One of our Problem Analysts will sit in a toilet cubicle if there's nowhere else to go. You need to get away from the problem periodically. Your brain can only take so much in one go. It takes some will power and you need to be careful not to appear to be wasting time, which is why sitting in a toilet cubicle is useful as it's a privilege that can hardly be denied.

Getting away from the immediate pressure can pay big dividends.

**Many of our Problem Analysts solve problems
as they drive home from the customer.**

Agreeing a time to give those interested an update on progress should help things.

Dealing with Disagreements

If a disagreement arises over the agreed Diagnostic Capture Plan, go back to the meeting room with the whiteboard.

**"Let's go back to the meeting room and
review the Action Plan in case it needs changing."**

Does everyone still agree with the details of the problem and the Diagnostic Capture Plan?

A Problem Analyst was asked by a network manager to determine the cause of slow network performance. He found that a heavy load was being generated by a group of engineers installing Windows onto PCs over the network. The network manager wanted to know if there were any other problems, but to determine this the engineers would need to stop what they were doing, which they weren't very happy about.

In this situation the best resolution is via straightforward negotiation. If that fails, escalate the issue to a higher level of management (but don't take this course if it can avoid it) and present each side of the argument in straightforward business terms:

- "If I am unable to complete my tests, the performance of the network will continue to be poor and this impacts the ability of your staff to do their job"

- "If we stop the engineers installing Windows it will delay completion of the XYZ project"

Don't start talking about 70% utilisation this and error rates that – it means nothing in business terms – but present the straightforward business impact. IT or business operational management can determine the highest priority issue, or maybe authorise overtime working for the engineers.

Beware of gremlins

Often people close to a problem will get irrational about it. Whilst looking at a network problem for a life assurance company, a server support engineer called our Problem Analyst over to look at an issue she had found. On the log of a number of servers was an error message indicating that the server had received short packets. She said that this had only been happening since a new network had been installed. The Problem Analyst explained why it was very unlikely to be a network infrastructure problem.

She said she understood but added:

"You don't understand. I know our network and it's different."

She was implying that it had a mind of its own. The Problem Analyst asked her if she had old server logs available. She did – going back to well before the new network was installed – and all contained the same error message regarding short packets. There had been a problem for at least four months before the new network was installed.

People under great pressure get ground down by repeated problems and can begin to think illogically.

Handling Complaints

When a Problem Solving Group messes up the Problem Manager and/or Problem Analyst may need to handle complaints. A very simple way to handle complaints is through five steps:

- Listen

- Sympathise

- Don't justify

- Plan a course of action

- Follow-through

The only point that needs expanding here is *Don't justify*. The customer (manager, user, colleague, etc.) may ask for an explanation of the actions taken. A possible response is:

"Bearing in mind the seriousness of the problems, let's get it resolved first and then meet to discuss the lessons we learned."

The complainant should be happy as the complaint has been heard and it will be dealt with.

Problems and Politics

Organisation Politics

It's difficult to know where to start with this issue. Large organisations are very political. Here are some experiences we have had at Advance7:

- A number of companies have tried to use us as a lever against suppliers to avoid payment for something

- We have been used by one department that is at war with another to prove a point

- Managers have rejected our findings as the outcome would damage the esteem of their department

- People have told us the outcome they want and then refused to pay us when the outcome was different

It can be very difficult to stay out of any politics. Whatever your role, you will often be asked to give an opinion on whether appropriate action was taken at an earlier stage of the problem. If you work in an end-user company you'll be aware of the politics and have your own way of handling the situation.

Stay out of it as much as possible, and even if someone has made a mistake handle the matter diplomatically. You may feel that you want to blame one supplier or another, particularly if you have been giving them a hard time, but don't. You don't know when you may need their help again.

Four tips to avoid political problems:

- Don't give an opinion on the effectiveness or capabilities of anyone

- Never disparage anyone or any piece of equipment

- Avoid any form of political discussion

- Use something like, "I only understand the technical aspects. I'm not qualified to give a business perspective"

Political games

We were asked by a manufacturing company to look at a problem affecting a group of users of a pair of very old file servers running unsupported software. The users worked in a drawing office and spent all day using a CAD application. The typical work pattern would be to start the CAD application, load a drawing, work on it all day, file it and go home.

The problem was that when they came to file it they no longer had a valid connection to the fileserver. The network group had virtually torn the network apart to try to discover the cause and had reached the conclusion that the problem was in the file server. The Server Platform Manager asked Advance7 to identify the cause of the problem.

The Server Platform Manager had insisted that the problem was being caused by 'killer' packets being sent out by some print servers that had been installed by the network group.

We were able to prove that there was no such 'killer' packet, and that the connection was being dropped due to a problem with the connection status mechanism in the file server.

It turned out that the Server Platform and Network Managers had been in dispute over a number of issues. As a result the Server Platform Manager would not accept our explanation and the issue had to be resolved by involving senior management.

Handling Suppliers

Building the Relationship

Getting the supplier on your side may be difficult if you work for an end-user company and the relationship with the supplier has gone a bit sour. A supplier may feel that you are just out to nail him.

If you have no former relationship with the supplier support staff you may have to win them over as they are sometimes wary of anyone calling themselves a Problem Manager or Problem Analyst. You need to make sure they understand that:

- You are not out to promote another supplier's equipment

- You won't make them look foolish – on the contrary …

- You need their help and probably won't be able to solve the problem without it

Establish a good working relationship with them at an early stage.

Getting Them Engaged

A common issue is that many suppliers are unwilling to give details of actions they want taken in writing. A simple but important question to ask is:

> **"If this does turn out to be a problem with your equipment what information would you need to pursue the problem?"**

About a third of suppliers don't have an answer, and say they will need to speak to the developers. A further third will tell you anything to get you off the phone but refuse to confirm any requirements in writing. The final third will give you clear guidance and are prepared to put it in writing.

Leave it to us

Sometimes sharing a Diagnostic Capture Plan with a supplier can result in a surprising outcome. We were investigating a problem with an email server and passed our DCP to the software manufacturer's support team. They said they believed there was a problem in their software and that they would take ownership of the problem. After several months of having the customer jump through all sorts of technical hoops they declared that they didn't know the cause but it was not their problem.

The Diagnostic Capture Plan is very useful here. You can email it to a supplier and it can be forwarded to anywhere within minutes. Using the Diagnostic Capture Plan in this way means that you are effectively talking directly to the developers, something that you can rarely do otherwise. There's no chance of misinterpretation of the situation after a lengthy phone conversation with an intermediary – it's there in front of them in black and white. Here are the actions you need to take:

- Talk to the supplier as early as you can. Explain who you are and what you are about. Get the name and email address of the correct contact.

- Follow-up to check that the recipient has read the Diagnostic Capture Plan.

- "Do you agree with the Problem Description?"

- "Do you agree with the planned actions?"

- "Do you need to send the Diagnostic Capture Plan to the developers?" "When will you send it?" "When will you have an answer?"

Always get the name of the person you are dealing with. You will need to keep on his or her tail all the time. Contact him at all the agreed times to check progress. Ask him if the developers need any further information or if they would like to speak to you directly.

In the defence of supplier support staff, they are often very overworked. Support is seen by some suppliers as either an easy way of making revenue or an evil that eats into profit. Manufacturers and their development staff are often focused on developing the next product and so can lose interest in solving problems with existing products. This, coupled with a similar emphasis all down the supply chain, means that support departments are often understaffed and rushed off their feet.

What Not To Do

We've worked with a number of customers that have tried to use a problem to beat up a supplier or wring more from them. A typical scenario goes something like this:

**IT Manager – "If this turns out to be their problem
they can have the damn equipment back."**

**Supplier – "We are not prepared to take the equipment back,
the warranty ran out 6 months ago."**

**Supplier – "If we fix this will we get
the maintenance business next year?"**

At first light it would appear that the IT Manager has the supplier over a barrel, but there are two problems:

1. If the supplier is threatened with some form of penalty if it's proved that their equipment is the cause of a problem you can be sure that they are not going to be too keen to help

2. If fixing of the problem is linked to next year's business and the salesman decides that he doesn't want the business the supplier may lose all interest in helping to resolve the problem

The key rules are:

- Distance the Problem Solving Group from any commercial aspects of the outcome of the problem

- Don't let the supplier mix the resolution of the problem with commercial issues

Escalation

When should you escalate a problem? There are five circumstances under which you will need to escalate a problem:

- No action from a colleague

- No action from a supplier and no commitment to action

- No agreed timetable or Action Plan

- Repeated failure to hit agreed dates

- Failure of the supplier to meet expectations / SLAs

Hopefully the escalation procedure within your own organisation is known and understood. Escalating an issue with a supplier is likely to be controlled by SLAs defined in a contract or terms of business. It is always useful to have these to hand if they favour your case. However, unexpected issues arise that perhaps are not covered by the agreed SLAs but require special consideration. If you are struggling to get support from a supplier, there are two routes available to you:

- Technical – Work up through the specialist, senior specialist, support manager, etc. Exhaust this route first.

- Sales – Use this route if the technical route fails.

Most suppliers are sales led and so the sales staff have a lot of clout. Check with interested parties (your manager, procurement staff, supplier managers, etc.) before you use this route. It's also advisable to tell the supplier support engineer that this is a serious problem and you need to escalate, taking care not to antagonise him:

"Jim, I need to escalate this problem because it's impacting us severely. I want to make sure you get all the resources you need. What's the best way to escalate the problem so that you can help us?"

Bearing in mind the pressures on support staff, someone is setting the support engineer's priorities. If he's been told to deal with you or your type of problem on a low priority basis you need to get his priorities changed. On the other hand, if he's leading you a dance he's likely to tell you that he will handle it and things should improve from that point on. Don't go around him unless you absolutely have to.

 Escalation through Sales

We identified a problem with a web load-balancer. Intermittently it would muddle HTTP headers and send the wrong cookies to a user.

We reported the problem to the supplier and asked for it to be dealt with as a Priority 1 problem since it meant that there was a possibility of young website users gaining access to Adult Content. The support staff said that they were under strict instructions to accept a problem as Priority 1 only if the box was 'down'.

We called the Account Manager and explained the issue. He immediately had the problem raised to Priority 1.

Appendix A – RPR Process Map

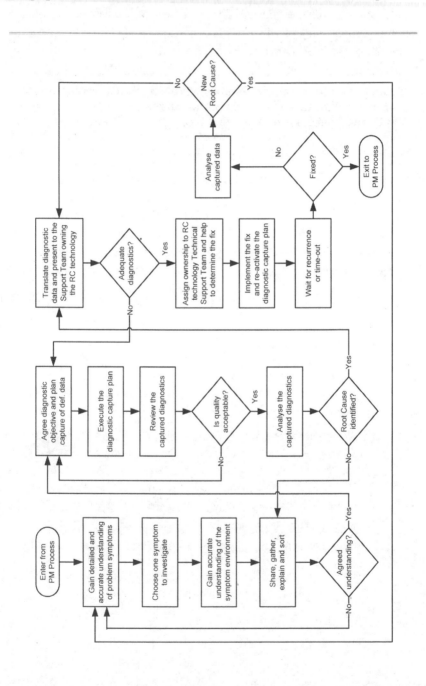

Appendix B – Useful Information

TCP/IP Essentials

IP

IP is a mechanism for passing small pieces of data (known as packets) from one computer to another via a network. Every IP packet has an IP header which contains useful information about the packet and its contents. Two important fields in the IP header are the Source Address (where the packet has come from) and the Destination Address (where the packet is going to).

An IP packet is a string of bytes laid out something like this:

	TTL	Protocol		Source IP Address	Destination IP Address	Higher Level Protocol & Data

As the packet crosses the network it is 'routed' to the correct destination. As a packet arrives at a router the destination address is checked against a routing table and the packet is sent on its way.

Figure 41   TCP/IP essentials

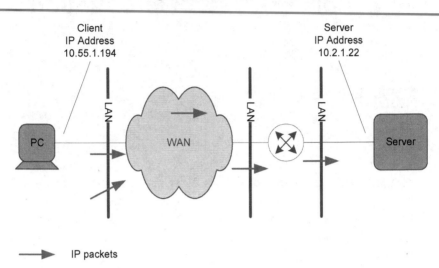

IP packets

The network maintains no knowledge of a relationship between each packet, it just makes its routing decisions on a packet-by-packet basis. It doesn't care what is in each packet and it doesn't inspect the TCP Header, it just passes the packet to the next router in the path from source to destination. As you might expect, the Source and Destination Addresses are swapped for packets travelling in the opposite direction.

TCP

When looking at a network application, such as a web application, there are two important processes:

- A client machine process – for a web application this might be Internet Explorer or Firefox

- A server process – the web server itself, perhaps IIS or Apache

TCP is a transport mechanism that guarantees the delivery of data from one process to another. It makes sure that all packets arrive safely and in the correct order. Unlike IP, TCP does keep track of the relationship between each packet.

An important concept is that of the TCP Port. Inside any one computer there will be many applications that communicate using TCP/IP. If the IP Destination Address gets a packet to the right computer, how does the packet get to the right process?

Figure 42 TCP/IP stack

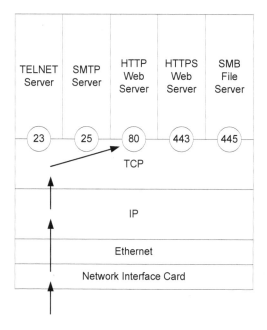

The TCP Header carries a TCP Source Port that indicates which process the packet[10] has come from, and a TCP Destination Port that indicates which process it is destined for. The TCP Port number for a service is usually fixed and well known (such as Port 80 for a web server). The client TCP Port number is chosen randomly and is said to be dynamic.

An important aspect of maintaining the relationship between a process sending packets through one TCP Port and a process receiving packets through another, is the concept of a TCP Connection.

---

[10] Strictly, a TCP message is called a segment, and a segment gets encapsulated with an IP packet. It's common, however, for the term packet to be used to mean any network message.

Whereas IP is like sending a Text Message (you click Send and hope the network will deliver it to the correct destination), TCP is more like making a phone call (you dial the number, someone answers and says hello, and you say hello back). Just like a phone network, TCP makes a connection between a client process and a server process.

Figure 43   TCP/IP connection sequence

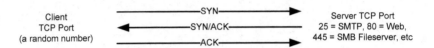

The connection is established by the client sending to the server an empty TCP packet with a special flag called SYN set. The server responds with two flags; SYN and ACK. To complete the process the client sends an empty packet with the ACK flag set and now the connection is made.

Think of a long piece of flexible hose, the openings at each end being the Ports and the hose representing the Connection. You push packets in one end and they come out of the other.

Every TCP packet has a TCP Sequence Number that increases each time data is sent along a TCP connection. It doesn't increase by one, but instead increases by a number the same as the length of the data in the previous packet.

Figure 44   TCP sequence numbers

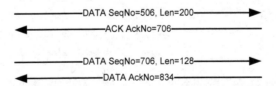

Acknowledgements (ACKs) may flow in the opposite directions to confirm safe reception of the data. Data in one direction can be acknowledged by data flowing in the opposite direction. The Sequence Number used in one direction has no relationship to the Sequence Numbers used in the opposite direction.

Figure 45 TCP acknowledgement

With a few exceptions, all applications use the TCP connection in a serial manner. For example, to open a file on an SMB server and read the contents the client will send an OPEN command[11], wait for the reply, and then send a READ command. This means that you can check the response time from a server merely by looking at the time difference between the command arriving at the server and the server sending the reply.

There are exceptions to this rule, and two common ones are:

A Citrix or Windows Terminal Server client sends keyboard strokes and mouse movements along a TCP Connection in one direction, and the server sends the screen updates in the opposite direction on the same Connection but there is no strict relationship between any of these packets.

A web browser will send a command to request a page on a connection and receive the page content on the same connection. It may then create more parallel TCP Connections to get imbedded images, style sheets, Javascript files, etc. This is done to speed up rendering of the page.

---

[11] In practice the SMB command used is NT Create with a Disposition of Open.

Appendix C – Worked Examples

Multi-Trace Correlation Worked Example

Problem Description

In this example we look at a problem facing a leisure company with branches all over the UK. The company has a centralised system to handle all aspects of branch management. The system is centred on a BizTalk server with a supporting database server, and is accessed in the branch through Internet Explorer and the HTTP protocol. For some transactions, the BizTalk server sends SQL requests to an MSDE database server in the branch.

The application menu includes an Appointments option to display one-on-one personal training sessions. Intermittently, displaying the appointments for the day took more than 10 seconds. The suspicion was that the problem is caused by the Wide Area Network that connects the branch to the Data Centre.

Figure 46   Multi trace correlation

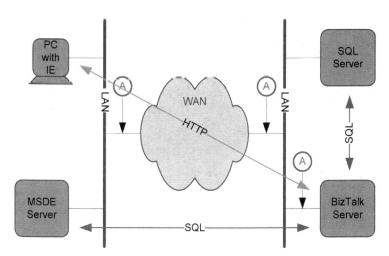

Actions

The approach to this problem was as follows:

- Three analysers were configured to capture network traffic at the remote branch, at the exit from the WAN into the Data Centre LAN and in and out of the BizTalk server.

- Alongside the application window we started a Windows Command box with a ping command with a data length of 101 bytes ready for sending to the BizTalk server.

- When the problem occurred the ping was sent.

- The analysers were then stopped.

- The PC's IP address was noted.

- The ping was found in the Analyser 1 trace. The HTTP GET command was evident immediately before the ping. The TCP sequence number for the GET request and the corresponding 200 OK reply was noted.

- The time difference between the GET request and 200 OK reply was noted to be 13.633952 seconds

- The Analyser 2 trace file was filtered to display packets from the PC in question.

- A search of the trace records was conducted using the TCP Sequence Number of the GET request. Packet header and content information was used to confirm that the correct packet had been found.

- The corresponding 200 OK reply was found.

- The time difference between the GET request and 200 OK reply was noted to be 13.553810 seconds

- The time attributable to the WAN was calculated by taking the Analyser 2 figure from that of Analyser 1 and found to be only 0.080142 seconds or approximately 80 ms.

- By filtering and searching the capture files from Analyser 3 the offending GET request was found. The request and its corresponding response then formed the start and end boundaries for analysis of the database interactions.

- Using data content from the HTTP stream (principally the Branch ID, and some of the data returned) the database interactions were identified in the Analyser 3 trace.

Findings

The following diagram gives an overview of the findings.

Figure 47 Breakdown of response time

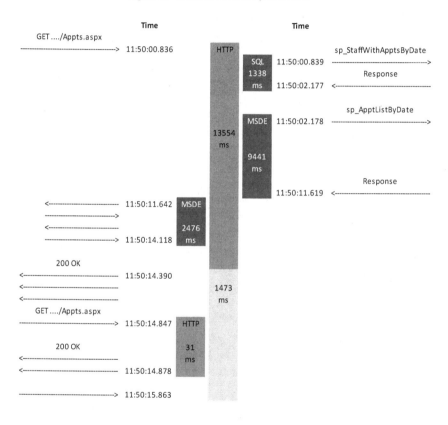

Summarising this, we see that the time breaks down as follows:

Figure 48 Time account

		Time Contribution (s)
User PC		-0.049
WAN		1.522
Web Server		
- Central DB	10.779	
- Branch DB	2.476	
- Other	0.000	
- Application	0.299	
		13.554
		15.027

This result looks slightly strange as the time in the User PC is a negative value. This is due to the fact that the user response time (15.027s) was measured with a stopwatch which wasn't very accurate. Although more complex analysis could be carried out to improve the accuracy it's unnecessary since the cause of the slow performance is quite obvious, and in practice this is usually the case.

The information provided using this technique is extremely powerful. In this example, two aspects were a complete surprise:

- The website developers did not expect the BizTalk server to access the branch MSDE server for the appointments transaction, and this was later found to be a coding mistake.

- The DBA believed that dbo.sp_ApptListByDate was no longer used and so he had not profiled its performance.

Resolution

The problem was resolved by commenting out the call to the MSDE database and tuning the Stored Procedure.

Timescales

Collection of the data, identification of the call to the Branch Database and confirmation that the network was not the cause of the problem, was achieved within a single working day.

Network Trace Correlation Worked Example

This Worked Example outlines the steps taken to diagnose a performance problem with an IBM mainframe application accessed via a 3270 terminal emulator and the SNA communications protocol. The SNA and 3270 terminal protocols are no longer widely used but much can be learned from this Worked Example as it demonstrates several key Supporting Techniques. The simplicity of the protocols also makes it an ideal example for rookie RPR practitioners.

Problem Description

The application under scrutiny here was a mainframe-based system, accessed via IBM 3270/SNA terminal protocol and used to process customer credit card information. Normally application response times were sub-second, but users reported that between 08:30 and 09:30 every morning response times were often greater than 5 seconds and sometimes greater than 30 seconds.

Symptom Environment

The system is hosted in a central Data Centre and used by around 3,000 staff at two remote contact centres. The application is accessed via 3270 terminal emulation software running on the user's PC. Architecturally the system consists of four Microsoft Host Integration Servers (HIS) split across 2 sites (2 servers at each site).

Figure 49   Contact centre network topology

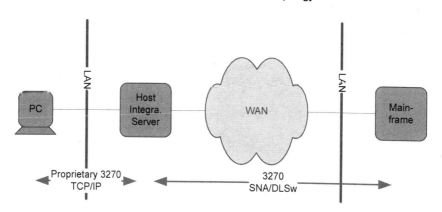

The user PC communicates with the HIS server via an encrypted proprietary protocol running over a TCP/IP connection. The HIS server communicates with the mainframe application over an SNA LU-LU session (similar to a TCP connection) using 3270/SNA over the DLSw (Data Link Switching) link level protocol.

An LU can be thought of as similar to a TCP Port i.e. the interface through which an application gains access to the network. In this LU-LU session we had the 3270 terminal represented by an LU in the HIS server on one side and the Mainframe application on the other.

The client software chooses one of the HIS servers at random each time the software is loaded and runs a script to login to the application. When connected the terminal emulation software displayed the LU name in use and this maps to a particular HIS server. Using this information IT support staff had determined that users experienced the response time problem no matter which HIS server they were connected to.

Diagnostic Boundaries

The following boundaries were identified to help determine our Diagnostic Capture Plan:

- The problem occurs for all users, although not at the same time

- The problem has only been reported at one contact centre

- The problem occurs during peak periods in the morning between 08:30 and 09:30

- The problem occurred no matter which HIS server was selected

Diagnostic Capture Plan (DCP)

We considered the end to end system as four functional units:

- The user PC and local LAN in Contact Centre 1

- The HIS Server in Contact Centre 1

- The LAN and WAN connecting the HIS server to the Data Centre

- The Data Centre LAN and all mainframe components

The initial objective was to determine how much time each of the functional units contributed to the total response time when the user experienced a response time of greater than 5 seconds. The basic plan was:

1. Install or configure appropriate tools to generate adequate Definitive Diagnostic Data

2. Locate ourselves near the users

3. Wait for a user to report a slow response time

4. Immediately send a marker to mark the diagnostic data

5. Capture transaction information i.e. data from the user's screen

6. Capture identification information such as userid, IP address and SNA LU name

7. Repeat steps 3 to 6 through the one-hour period of the problem

We decided to use network analysers to capture Definitive Diagnostic Data as these would be non-disruptive. We set network analysers in place to capture in three locations thereby covering the interfaces between the functional units.

Figure 50 Contact centre functional units

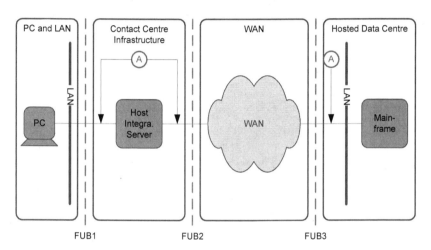

FUB1   FUB2   FUB3

(A)   Network Analyser

The functional unit boundaries are represented by FUB1, FUB2, etc.

The random selection of HIS servers by PCs in Contact Centre 1 meant that to be certain to capture all PC to HIS sessions we needed to install network analysers in Contact Centre 2. However, we decided that the frequency of the problem was such that users connected to any server would experience the problem eventually we decided to capture in Contact Centre 1 only.

To simplify the correlation of the encrypted proprietary PC to HIS traffic with the 3270 HIS to Mainframe traffic we used an analyser with two network interfaces to capture traffic for each HIS interface. In this way we knew that both network streams would be captured with a common timestamp, avoiding the need to correct for time sync differences.

The network analyser in the Data Centre was situated at the interface with the WAN. As traffic captured at FUB2 and FUB3 should match at an SNA level, approximate time synchronisation was thought to be sufficient to match traces and determine the LAN/WAN delay between these two points.

We decided to use simple ping markers to mark the PC to HIS server trace each time the problem occurred. To differentiate each occurrence of the problem we used ping markers with differing lengths. The pings were to be sent from a spare PC located on a desk close to the users who were reporting the problem. The ping marker needed to be sent to both HIS servers in Contact Centre 1.

Execution of the DCP

Network analysers were installed and monitor ports were configured to enable their connection to the network. Work started early one Monday morning and the workflow ran like this:

1. Our Problem Analyst manually synchronised the analysers in Contact Centre 1 to the speaking clock and then started them capturing

2. A network engineer from the in-house team manually synchronised the analyser in the Data Centre to the speaking clock and then started them capturing based on instructions we had emailed to him

3. The Problem Analyst relocated himself to the area of the users and explained to the users how he was helping to diagnose the poor performance problem

4. The Problem Analyst recorded the name, userid, IP address and LU name of eight workstations to be monitored

5. A local IT support engineer logged in the spare PC

6. The Problem Analyst started a Cmd window on the spare PC and typed the first ping command (ping -l 101 ....) but did not send it

7. The Problem Analyst asked the users to report any response time greater than five seconds to him immediately it happened and not to continue working until he had given the go ahead (a matter of about a 30 seconds delay)

As soon as a user reported a slow response time, the Problem Analyst:

8. Sent the ping marker to both HIS servers in Contact Centre 1

9. Recorded the time of the problem (taken from the spare PC clock), the user name and the transaction type that was being executed together with variable data that appeared in the transaction response i.e. what was on the screen after the problem

10. Recorded the response time, which for this particular terminal emulator appeared in a status line on the screen

11. Gave the user the go-ahead to continue

12. Recorded all information in his notebook

13. Set up a new ping with a new length (ping -l 102 ....) on the spare PC ready for the next problem

14. Waited for the next problem

Some examples were deemed to be poor quality since:

- The response time was thought to be atypical because of some user action

- The problem was reported too late to generate timely markers

- The user had moved on to another session rather than wait for us to attend and record their details

We terminated the DCP when we had captured 10 clean examples of the performance problem.

Analysis

The plan was to analyse the data on a problem occurrence by occurrence basis as follows:

1. Find the marker for the slow response time in the PC to HIS network traces, and hence determine which HIS server the user was connected to at the time of the problem

2. Work backwards through the trace to determine the start and end of the slow transaction

3. Calculate the 'on the wire' response time by determining the difference in the timestamps of the first network packet of the transaction and the last network packet

4. Compare the 'on the wire' response time with that of the response time displayed on the screen. If they are approximately equal we can conclude that the problem was not within the user PC or LAN infrastructure

5. Confirm that any slow response time is not due to TCP retransmission of data for this transaction that would indicate a network infrastructure problem or overload

6. For each particular occurrence of the problem, correlate the PC to HIS trace with the HIS to Mainframe trace – more detail on this below

7. Compare the 'on the wire' response time for the PC to HIS session as per above with the 'on the wire' response time measured in the HIS to Mainframe trace – if they are approximately equal we can conclude that the problem was not within the HIS server

8. Confirm that any slow response time is not due to DLSw retransmission of data for this transaction that would indicate a network infrastructure problem or overload in the contact centre

9. Compare the 'on the wire' response time for the HIS to Mainframe trace as per above with the 'on the wire' response time measured by the trace captured in the Data Centre. If they are approximately equal we can conclude that the problem was not within the WAN

10. Confirm that any slow response time is not due to DLSw retransmission of data for this transaction that would indicate a network infrastructure problem or overload in the Data Centre

Results

Several examples of problem occurrences were studied and the following results were typical of the response times at each FU boundary

Response Times at each FU Boundary		
FUB1	FUB2	FUB3
Transaction 1 22.7s	0.058s	0.032s

Because the response time measured at FUB1 was almost identical to that displayed in the status line of the user's screen we were able to conclude that the problem was not caused by the PC or local LAN. The response times measured at the HIS server SNA interface and in the Data Centre were also almost identical, and so this proved that there was no problem with the LAN/WAN infrastructure. The response time measured at the Data Centre was sub-second and totally acceptable, and so the problem did not appear to be within the Mainframe or local infrastructure.

The difference in the response times measured each side of the HIS server proved conclusively that the excessive response times were due to serious delays inside the HIS server.

Diagnostic Data Translation

To enable the toohnology owner to resolve the root cause, it is important to present the evidence for the root cause as clearly and concisely as possible.

We presented the findings to the HIS Server support team who subsequently engaged Microsoft Technical Support. We packaged the sample traces (filtered for particular users) together with notes explaining the diagnostic markers and identifying the key trace events, and emailed them across to the Microsoft Engineer.

Microsoft quickly concurred that there was a performance problem within the HIS Server.

Correlation

Matching the traces taken at FUB2 and FUB3 is quite straightforward since we should simply see the same IP packets (assuming no retransmissions).

Figure 51   Contact centre data correlation

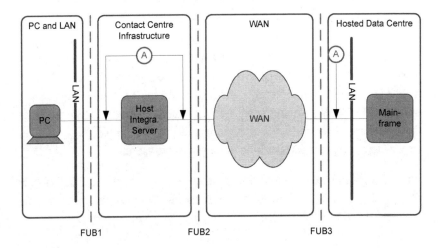

FUB1   FUB2   FUB3

(A)   Network Analyser

Correlating the interactions seen at FUB1 and FUB2 is more difficult since:

- Two different protocols are being used across the two boundaries – proprietary over TCP/IP and 3270/SNA over DLSw

- There may not be a one-to-one relationship between the packets at each boundary

- The packets at one boundary are encrypted

As both TCP and SNA are connection-orientated protocols, i.e. there is a permanent transport-level connection between client and server, we believed that once the user had completed the application login that there would be a permanent relationship between the TCP session and the SNA session.

We correlated the trace entries each side using the following procedure:

1. Find the marker sent following a slow response time in the FUB1 traces

2. Filter the traces selecting entries for the affected user only and save the filtered example

3. Filter the trace further to select only traffic to the HIS service TCP port in use and displaying only traffic with a TCP Length greater than zero

4. By studying long time gaps between data packets to the PC and subsequent packets from the PC (probably signifying user think time) identify the end of one transaction and the start of the next

5. Identify the pattern of traffic flow for a transaction

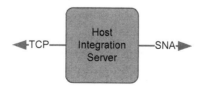

Figure 52 HIS transport protocols

6. Using the start and end time of each good transaction as time boundaries, study the traffic flows in the trace collected at FUB2 for the same HIS server

7. For each good transaction identified in steps 4 to 6, focus on SNA packets flowing to the Mainframe just after the first packet from the PC to the HIS server, and the last packet from the Mainframe to the HIS server that occurs just before the last packet from the HIS server to the PC

8. Repeat step 7 two or three times until you have determined the mapping from the User PC IP address to the SNA LU number

9. Using the IP address to LU number match, map out the traffic flows each side of the HIS server for a slow transaction bearing in mind that a packet from the PC to the HIS server will be translated into a packet from the HIS server to the Mainframe and vice versa

It's always useful to draw the data flow to visualise the interactions as shown below.

Figure 53 Contact centre data correlation

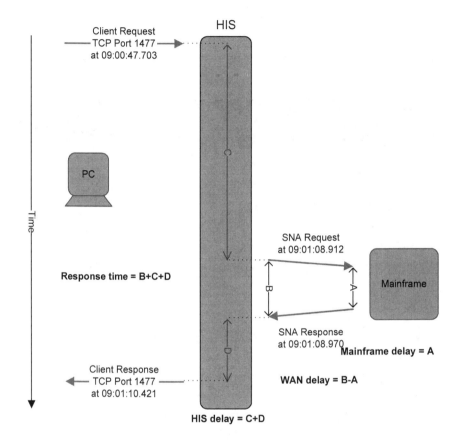

An alternative method to establish the mapping of IP address to LU name is possible if the trace includes the establishment of the user's connection to the Mainframe application (known as an LU-LU BIND). The BIND contains the user's LU name, which is also shown in the status line of the 3270 emulation window. Search for this BIND in the SNA trace and find the corresponding TCP connection in the PC to HIS server trace.

Analysis Detail

In this section we show how the network trace data was analysed using the popular Wireshark open source network analyser. The information gathered by the Problem Analyst at the time of the problem was as follows:

Time	Marker Length	Client IP	Delay (sec)	Last Action	LU
09:01	303	192.168.4.2	22.7	Enter	HISLU3049

From the LU name we determined that the user was connected to the HIS server CC1HISA. In fact, this fact wasn't initially certain and so the correlation technique detailed above was used as a cross check.

Client-side (IP) Captures

To extract the slow transaction from the trace files taken at FUB1 we applied the following Wireshark filter to our capture file:

(ip.addr==192.168.4.2 && tcp.len>0) or (icmp && ip.addr==192.168.4.10)

This reduces the trace to show just TCP data packets plus the ping marker. Paging through the trace file to the time of the reported problem we find the ping marker (ICMP Echo Request) at frame 300 – see screenshot below.

Figure 54   TCP flow Wireshark summary

```
296 09:00:35.702071 0.000001   192.168.4.200      192.168.4.2        1477
297 09:00:47.703292 12.001221   192.168.4.2        192.168.4.200      3840
298 09:01:10.421644 22.718352   192.168.4.200      192.168.4.2        1477
299 09:01:10.421906 0.000262    192.168.4.200      192.168.4.2        1477
300 09:01:28.935936 18.514030   192.168.4.10       192.168.4.200
301 09:01:28.936145 0.000209    192.168.4.200      192.168.4.10
```

The packet highlighted in frame 298 is a response 22.7 seconds after the request in frame 297 – which correlates with the information displayed on the user client.

We therefore used frames 297 and 298 as our time boundary – we knew that anything impacting the response times occurred within this timeframe, i.e. before this time was too early for the client request, after this time the client had already received its response from the HIS server.

This shows that the majority of the delay is occurring outside of the client, i.e. in the HIS server, WAN or mainframe.

To determine if the client request was passed from the HIS server to the mainframe, and was responded to in a timely fashion, we needed to match the IP request with an SNA request. This was made more difficult due to the encrypted nature of the IP side requests. Our earlier determination of the boundary start and end times, and the fact that both the client-side and the mainframe-side traces are time-stamped via a common clock, overcame the encryption issues.

In an SNA packet the equivalent of a client TCP port number is the LU Number. To filter the trace data correctly we needed to determine the LU Number for the user who experienced the slow response time. In this case the network analysers had been running for a long period and so had captured the initial login to the application. Therefore we were able to search for the HSILU3049 LU name in the trace data and found that it related to LU number 49 on CC1HISA.

We then filtered the mainframe-side (FUB2) trace using the following filter expression:

(eth[20] == 49 || eth[21] == 49) && (llc.control.ftype == 0x0000)

This filter expression selects all SNA packets for LU Number 49. The llc.control.ftype setting ensures that we filter out LLC control and acknowledgement frames. We paged through the trace to the start of the time boundary established from the client-side trace. The resulting trace entries looked like this:

Figure 55 SNA flow Wireshark summary

[illegible]	[illegible]	[illegible]	[illegible]	[illegible]	[illegible]	[illegible]	IPX
232	09:01:08.912263	33.220719	0049	0001			SNA
233	09:01:08.970356	0.058093	40404005.404040054040	039040f1.c31140c11311	0x4040	0x50e6	IPX
234	09:02:00.186685	51.216329	0049	0001			SNA
235	09:02:00.334627	0.147942	1140e31d.f0000011406d	039000f1.c31140c1e6c1	0xc7c2	0xc7d5	IPX

NB: Interpretation of some of the frames as IPX is a Wireshark problem – the frames are in fact all SNA.

This trace shows an SNA Request packet (frame 232) and a Reply within 60ms (frame 233). Quite obviously there is no problem with the WAN or mainframe service.

Conclusion

Pulling together the two traces we see the following events:

- 09:00:47.703292 – a request from the PC arrives at the HIS server

- 09:01:08.912263 – the HIS server sends the user request to the mainframe

- 09:01:08.970356 – the reply from the mainframe arrives at the HIS server

- 09:01:10.421644 – the HIS server sends the reply to the user PC

This shows that there is a 21.208971-second delay in the HIS server forwarding the request to the mainframe, and a 1.451288-second delay in the HIS server forwarding the reply the user PC.

Appendix D – Responsibilities

Allocation of roles and responsibilities will of course vary from business to business but here we provide a guide.

Leadership in the investigation and diagnosis of a problem using RPR typically falls to two people:

- Facilitator – a Problem, Incident, Recovery or Service Delivery Manager

- Lead Problem Analyst – a senior 3rd Line support person

In smaller organisations one senior technical person is likely to carry out both roles.

In larger organisations the complexity of reporting structures means that marshalling resources and communicating with the business are more time consuming. In this case a dedicated Facilitator is very useful to liaise with technical groups, managers and business units.

The Problem Solving Group (PSG) should comprise:

- Facilitator

- Lead Problem Analyst

- Application owner

- 3rd Line support people from each team that owns components of the system

- Support staff from the suppliers of components that may be causing the problem

- A representative from the business

Responsibilities on a step-by-step basis are:

Process Step	Responsible
1.01 – Understand the problem	Lead Problem Analyst
1.02 – Choose one symptom	Lead Problem Analyst in conjunction with business managers
1.03 – Understand the symptom environment	Lead Problem Analyst
1.04 – Share, gather, explain and sort information	PSG Workshop arranged by the Facilitator Workshop led by the Lead Problem Analyst
1.05 – Agreed understanding?	All members of the PSG
2.01 – Plan the capture of definitive diagnostics	All members of the PSG agree the diagnostic objective All members of the PSG agree the outline of the DCP Lead Problem Analyst and technical support people agree the detail of the DCP The Facilitator circulates the DCP to interested parties
2.02 – Execute the Diagnostic Capture Plan	Lead Problem Analyst, technical support people and business representatives
2.03 – Quality check the captured data	Lead Problem Analyst

2.04 – Is data quality acceptable?	Lead Problem Analyst
2.05 – Analyse the captured data	Problem Analyst(s)
2.06 – Root cause identified?	Lead Problem Analyst
3.01 – Translate diagnostic data	Problem Analyst(s)
3.02 – Adequate diagnostics?	Lead Problem Analyst
3.03 – Work on a fix	Technical support people with input from the Lead Problem Analyst
3.04 – Implement fix and reactivate capture	Technical support team to implement the fix Lead Problem Analyst to reactivate the DCP
3.05 – Await a recurrence or timeout	All
3.06 – Is the problem fixed?	Lead Problem Analyst with technical support people
3.07 – Re-analyse the captured data	Problem Analyst(s)
3.08 – New root cause?	Lead Problem Analyst

Index

Further Information

Author

Paul Offord has had a 33-year career in the IT industry that includes roles in hardware engineering, software engineering and network management. Prior to founding Advance7 in 1989, he worked for IBM, National Semiconductor and Hitachi Data Systems.

Paul is now the Development Director at Advance7 and has been pivotal in the development of the RPR® Method. He is a respected speaker on the subject of problem diagnosis and delivers RPR training both in the UK and internationally.

Paul is a Certified IT Professional and a Fellow of the British Computer Society.

Advance7

Founded in 1989, Advance7 is an independent consultancy specialising in issues of IT performance and stability.

As well as delivering RPR® training and deployment services, Advance7 helps its clients diagnose difficult enterprise, Internet and cloud problems through an IT troubleshooting service called REACT®.

Advance7 has a rolling research and development programme to make sure that RPR and its Supporting Techniques keep pace with new technologies and changes in the IT environment.

Advance7 also operates the RPR Practitioner, RPR Master Practitioner and RPR Certified Trainer accreditation schemes.